RURAL LEADERSHIP IN INDIA

A Study of Emerging Trends in Democratic vs. Authoritarian Leadership

RURAL LEADERSHIP IN INDIA

A Study of Emerging Trends in Democratic vs. Authoritarian Leadership

V. Lalini

GIAN PUBLISHING HOUSE
New Delhi-110002

GIAN PUBLISHING HOUSE
4-C Ansari Road, Daryaganj
New Delhi 110 002

ISBN 81-212-0333-3

PRINTED IN INDIA

Published by Mrs. Gayatri Garg for Gian Publishing House New Delhi - 110 002.

Laser Typeset by Reliant Graphics B-501, Ansal Chamber-I, Bhikaji Cama Place New Delhi - 110066

Printed at Goyal Offset Printers, Delhi.

PREFACE

Leadership has played a vital role in the affairs of men since the earliest recorded history. It is an ancient art and requires constant attention. This is particularly required in a society, like ours, which is passing through a cultural transition characterised by a number of changes in social, economic and political life of the people. This social transformation is because of a planned change, and as a result of certain natural forces.

After independence the government of India launched a number of programmes of planned change to realise the qualitative improvement of socio-economic life of its people by self-help mutual help through the existing political systems. In pursuance of our planned social change, many forces and factors have been at work. Democratic planning visualised in India, presents specific difficulties, which are not common to other developing countries. Democratic processes here are complex as the conflicting pulls of traditional ideology are apt to generate friction and slow down the pace of change.

The social scientist is very often struck by a series of paradoxes while evaluating the nature of changes that have taken place in Indian society. One of the important reasons for such paradoxes is the communication-system built between policy makers and the rural masses through different intermediate agencies. Rural leaders form a strong link between the policy makers and governmental machinery on one hand, and the rural masses on the other; and many of our policies and programmes are translated into action only through this segment of rural community.

Social scientists evinced keen interest in the study of rural leadership, for the obvious reasons that the achievement of the targets for social change and effective implementation of programmes for development and planned change in most of the developing countries is largely dependent on the quality of leaders i.e. their desire and ability to blaze new path, the extent of their commitment to democratic values. In a social climate which is peculiar, paradoxical and, at times, paranoid as ours, success of any programme for development depends on the leaders, whom the community allows to assume position of great political power, their participation and their ability to secure the participation of the people in the programme.

It has been often felt that many policies framed at the top are not implemented either due to the communication gap that exists between the policy makers and the executors of the policy or due to distorted communication generating "noise" in the communication channel. Unless the rural leaders who from a link between policy-makers and rural masses are psychologically predisposed in favour of those policies and commit themselves to implement such policies, it is difficult to shape the destiny of the nation. In this context it is considered essential to examine the socio-psychological background of rural leaders with special reference to their democratic attitude.

Most of the studies on rural leadership have either dealt with the over-all social implications of the emerging leadership or to relate the socio-economic background as the determinant of leadership pattern. It is also to be noted that most of these studies are confined to a single village or a group of villages, dealing with one or two aspects of leadership, and comparing those findings with that of non-leaders. With few exceptions little attention has been given to study the degree of exposure to mass media and extension agency contact, levels of aspiration, the levels of social awareness, and the democratic vs authoritarian attitude. Further, little attention has been given to such studies of leadership in Andhra Pradesh. What is required is understanding and interpretation of various aspects of leadership in many villages to have a clear perception about the background (social, educational, psychological) of the leaders who play a crucial role in carrying message to rural masses.

Hence, the present study is an attempt to understand the nature and the pattern of emerging leadership in rural India. This study is based on the empirical data of rural communities of Telangana villages of Andhra Pradesh as following pages sufficiently testify to.

I owe a deep sense of gratitude to my teachers who have combined encouragement with valuable guidance and intelligent criticism throughout the course of this study. I acknowledge all those friends who have been associated with this work in number of ways and who made this effort meaningful. A special word of thanks is due to the U.G.C., which has enabled me to carry on this study, by awarding a research fellowship.

V. Lalini

CONTENTS

LIST OF TABLES

1

INTRODUCTION

This research aims at identifying the emerging leadership pattern in rural India and, examining the influence of a few selected social, educational and cultural factors on the attitudes of the rural leaders towards the processes of democratization. The significance of the study lies in the fact that the success of our democracy—towards which many programmes are directed depends on the pattern of emerging leadership and their socio-cultural background which might determine their attitudes towards these programmes.

Viewed from a historical background, the role played by the leaders in any civilization cannot be over-emphasized. The people providing leadership in the spheres of statesmanship, arts, culture and science have embellished many a great civilization of the past. David McClelland, pointed out with singular felicity in his book *The Achieving Society* that no civilization could survive a dearth of leaders who could stimulate the people to creativity.[1] In fact the downfall of the Egyptian, Greek, Roman or the Byzantine civilizations were not due to the marauding hordes of savages, but due to a sudden void in the sphere of leadership. In the absence of leaders who could coalesce the efforts of the people for progress and advancement of life, these civilizations gave up the fight for human cause and folded up. In the light of this revealing historical perspective the significance of the role of the leader in a developing country like ours needs no special emphasis.

India attained independence after 200 years of British subjugation and people are committed to an honourable institution *i.e.* democracy. Implicit in the proper functioning of this novel political ideology *i.e.* democracy, in this country is a proper comprehension of its challenges and commitments by the people. Therefore, in our endeavour to achieve this effect, the role of the leaders in the present context of our new social order cannot be amply and effectively stated.

Thus the people of this country are in dire need of leaders who not only understand the philosophy and the problems of democracy but also incorporate democratic attitude, conscientize the masses, and prepare them for an entirely new concept of living.

The history of India reveals that the people of this country had always been subjected to a kind of autocratic rule—be it a village headman, a king or a foreign tyrant. At many points of crisis, in Indian history, persons with altruistic ideology and social commitment had emerged as leaders and led the people to a better social life.[2] Retrospection reveals that most, if not all of the leaders in our history, were charismatic—charishma stemmed out of different causes, fear, respect and magical capacities, to solve the human problems.

It is interesting to note that the biggest flood of leaders occurred in our country during the nationalist movement in all fields—political, economic and cultural life of the people. The contribution of the great men like Tilak, Tagore, Raja Ram Mohan Roy and the all-round champion of the human cause, the father of the nation Mahatma Gandhi are to be noted especially in this context.[3] Therefore nostalgic attitude of millions of the people of this country and the myriad of references by press; all reveal the seemingly unfathomable morass where the want of dedicated and committed leaders is all pervasive. It is really ironical that this country which had produced leaders of the calibre of Tilak, Gandhi, Bose and Nehru should now grope in darkness for the benevolent hands of such leaders who can shape the destiny of this country, preparing the masses for an order to which we are committed.

There is a widespread feeling that, even after three decades of independence, 40 per cent of the people in this country live below poverty line plunged in the ignorance of the simplest economic facts. The country is caught up in a state of affairs to which the social scientists refer to as "Soft State", which stands out as a significant feature among other conditions that together make a country under-developed.[4] This does not mean however, that there are no leaders of national eminence who can lead the masses out of this morass. The fact remains that they are limited in number and are not in proportion to the magnitude and the multitude of the problems confronted by the nation. Therefore, the social scientists express their concern in their earnest desire to see that the situation does not drift and crash against the future.It is with this concern the present investigation is undertaken. It endeavours to make an empirical investigation of the social, educational and psychological background of the emerging leaders with a view to offering certain policy implications for education with special reference to its role in promoting such leadership.

For such an investigation it is necessary to understand the meaning and the dynamics of leadership. A survey of researches in social sciences on the problem indicates that the dynamics of leadership, its social origin and social consequences have always fascinated sociologists, social psychologists, political scientists and historians and the concepts of leader and leadership are defined variously by various social scientists. For instance, leadership has been defined by Fairchild as the act of organising and directing the interests and activities of a group of persons, as associated in some project or enterprise, by a person who develops their co-operation through securing and maintaining their voluntary approval of the ends and methods proposed and adopted in their association.[5]

Gibb has defined leadership as that aspect of role differentiation by which all or a large number of group members make use of individual contribution which they perceive to have value in bringing the group towards its goals.[6] Leadership is regarded as an activity of influencing people to co-operate 'towards some goal which they come to find desirable.[7] It has also been considered "a relation between an individual and a group, built around some common interest and behaviour as directed or determined by the leader".[8]

With the above definitions, two essential aspects in the leadership relation can be identified. The identification of a common purpose or goal and the ability to influence others to cooperate. A leader occupies a special status in the group. He is considered to be the central figure by all the members of the group who find in the qualities which can help them to achieve the desired goals.

The contemporary social scientists are presently interested in the functional aspect of leadership[9] which is being considered as a function of the group. This has necessitated the study of new dimensions of leadership, such as leadership behaviour, leadership action and interaction between leaders and non-leaders.[10]

Social Structure and Leadership

In this context it is to be noted that Indian society for centuries has been organised under the influence of traditional value orientations, like "Hierarchy" and "Pluaralism", manifesting in social inequalities, caste- based social stratification and rigid social mobility. The socio-cultural climate generated out of such social conditions, with a few exceptions, eliminated the possibilities of the rise of leaders from the lower sections of the society. People belonging to the upper strata of the society, by virtue of their ascribed status, played a vital role in social, political, economic and cultural aspects of Indian life. Haiman observed that the traditional leadership was based on seniority in age and inherited status.[11]

Therefore, to understand leadership pattern, particularly in rural set-up, it is necessary to know the social stratification of a community, which itself is a form of distribution of power among the members of the community.

Caste, status and occupation in traditional Indian villages were inter-woven and leadership position was confined to such privileged few, who enjoyed a higher rank position in the caste and occupational hierarchies. The hierarchy of caste determined the line of influence and control in the villages.[12]

Thus, the community power was concentrated in the hands of a few higher castes and land owning groups, who could exercise power to suit their whims and conveniences. In short, in the traditional village order the power was based on ascriptive order determined by birth.[13] Sacredness, ritualism, faith and ascribed status were considered to be the important aspects of traditional leadership. The traditional order in the Indian villages was given such a high valuation that it almost becomes sacrosanct.[14]

Traditional societies emphasised on system maintenance *i.e.* on the regularisation of various forces and ascribed roles to ensure the status quo. In such a value system, the leader's position was acquired by those whose ascribed role was held superrior or dominant in terms of inter-segmental relationships.[15] In the traditional social structure leaders by and large were conservative and traditional in outlook, fatalist in attitude and influenced strongly by the basic value inherent in the community structure.[16] Their ideology and function in society was more tradition reinforcing than oriented to structural changes or cultural innovation. Most of them lacked initiative, drive and interest in the new activities for the betterment of villages and confined their roles to the traditional authoritarian pattern.[17] A review of literature reveals that the leadership structure was, thus, by and large static, in the sense that there was little room for mobility, change, innovation or improvisation. The situation did not help the process of modernisation, particularly in rural India, where these leaders served as a 'reference groups' to the masses.

India, like any other developing country, is engaged in the stupendous task of modernizing itself. The existence of the traditional order for many centuries necessitated on our country's part a planned, quick and determined effort to initiate the process of social mobilization.[18] It has embarked upon a conscious programme of social change, and is attempting to build up a sound economic structure and a strong democratic edifice.

Though the importance of planning for carrying out the task of economic and social transformation had been emphasised in India from the early thirties of the 20th century, concrete steps have been initiated only after the achievement of independence.[19]

Many programmes have been developed to realise the social and economic development of the country within the broad framework of the national policies so that small communities can be absorbed into the stream of national progress.

It is with this realisation that the three tier democratic structure of local self government referred to as Panchayati Raj was introduced to make people self-reliant and to involve them in decision making. But contrary to the objectives of Panchayati Raj, which was started on the principle of democratization and which aimed at maximising people's participation and involvement in the developmental activities in rural India, it has led to the emergence of novel forms of political tensions and conflicts in rural areas.[20] Further, it has provided a new framework for political and caste struggles between rival landlords, jealous of their prestige and determined to maintain and if possible to strengthen their power network.[21]

It has been pointed out by a number of scholars that the implementation of the Panchayati Raj has further strengthened the caste system. Srinivas[22] in his study on *Caste in Modern India* observes that the power and activity of caste has increased in proportion as political power passed increasingly to the people from the rulers and the establishment of Panchayati Raj has given a new fillip to caste. .

A survey conducted by Sirsikar revealed that the rural politics tended to become more competitive than constructive and the rural leaders who were well-to-do peasantry class, with an agricultural background, displayed an increasing power consciousness.[23] Politics threatens to become more competitive than constructive and ideology would seem to count less than power consideration.[24]

In spite of the several social, economic and political reforms, it is widely felt that masses in general were exploited for personal gain by people who have economic, social and political power. Myrdal's statement that "while the opportunities for large scale exploitation opened up by the soft state are, of course, only at the disposal of the upper class, even persons quite low on the social ladder often find such opportunities for petty gains"[25] appears to be quite relevant to our rural life even today.

Sirsikar's remark "though maximum efforts are made, and variety of institutions are established, democratization of power involving a democratic society has yet to take place"[26] is true even today. Therefore, no society can be described as democratic for introducing the developmental programmes on a democratic basis if its fundamental approach is not democratic, if it is open philosophically but managed by people with narrow outlook, if it commits to do away with traditional social barriers but restricts and continues with its impoverished traditional, narrow, socialization methods, if it takes many avenues for progress but creates difficulties in achieving truth.

Therefore, our attempts during the past three decades, to achieve economic and social development in consonance with the establishment of a "socialistic pattern of society within the framework of a political democracy", our efforts to realise political, economic and social equality in the society, our endeavour for social uplift of traditionally underprivileged sections of the society, our programmes like promoting adult education, orientation for family planning, agriculture know-how, the knowledge about land reforms have not yielded adequate results.

While it is difficult to present a realistic picture of the existing conditions in our rural communities, one can safely argue that the sense of apathy and indifference seem to be the general character of the masses, and rural leaders are no exception.

The experiences during the last thirty years have amply proved that mere establishment of a large variety of institutions will not ensure democratization in this counrty, unless we infuse a real democratic spirit into the day-to-day working of these institutions. In view of such paradoxical situation confronted by the nation,the 'role of a leader' in India assumes a very vital dimension, and calls for a challenging task not only to understand the possibility and desirability of changes but also to discharge one's social obligation to justify his role as a leader of the masses. In the absence of a committed leadership it may, further, weaken our social conditions and pose a threat to our democracy.

Therefore, in the existing conditions we must have such promising persons as leaders, who are fully committed to democratic values, who blaze new paths of thought and action, and who enthuse, inspire, and influence persons in such a manner as can influence their actions and generally even their feelings and thoughts.

It is also to be noted that the process of modernisation and democratization requires secular, radical, rational and development-oriented leaders.[27] Inkles observes that modern leaders should have the qualities such as : (1) openness to new experiences,(2) independence from authority, (3) belief in efficacy of science and medicine, (4) ambition for one self and one's children to achieve high occupational, educational and political goals, (5) strong interest and active participation in civil and community affairs and local politics, (6) possession of information about the national and international news.[28]

While a leader is expected to be endowed with such broad qualities of life, a rural leader has a special task to perform. He should initiate the programmes of development to the rural community and create conditions where the villagers could aspire for higher standards of life. Leaders are needed to promote a reorientation of outlook and acceptance of new values among people. Therefore, the leaders in the rural Indian villages, in the present context, must have qualities such as receptivity to changes, readiness to implement new ideas, risk-taking ability, high level of aspirations, high degree of socio-cultural awareness.[29]

The present study has been designed, therefore, with a view to examining the pattern of emerging leadership in rural India, involving some of these variables. The significance of these variables can be viewed against a background of Indian socio-cultural life presented in the following pages.

Socio-Cultural Life of Indian People

India is a new nation and an old society with long history of culture and civilization. While it is difficult to present the detailed account of the socio-cultural life of the people in terms of its genesis and evolution and widespread practices, an attempt is made here to present a few salient aspects of rural Indian life which helps the reader to comprehend the rural socio-cultural climate.

Religion and spiritualism is one of the dominant themes of Indian culture.[30] The religious outlook of the rural people overwhelmingly dominated their intellectual, emotional, and practical life.[31]

People were under the influence of traditional Indian values, like belief in teleological order of the universe, doctrine of Karma, and transcendentalism.[32] Such socio-cultural forces of Indian community have contributed for the prevalence of many a social evil. The traditional philosophy, which has been transmitted from its ancient past to the present day through folk ways, epics, traditions, customs, and informal socialization processes, still dominates the ways of living of the people. People in rural areas are usually deeply committed to certain principles of rural life, in spite of the fact that they are contradictory to our constitutional goals and process of democratization.

Social evils such as, caste hierarchy, sex discrimination, male ascendancy, male supremacy, purity and pollution, bonded labour, child marriages, practice of untouchability, traditional credit system still exist today and are widely practised by a large number of people. They are the dominant characteristics of Indian social order and in spite of many developmental programme they continue to act as very strong obstacles in the process of modernization.

In this context the leaders who form the link between the masses and the nation have to play a crucial role in educating the masses. For this, the leaders should have not only a positive orientation towards the changes, national ideologies, and politics but also influence the masses to have a change of outlook.[33]

It is difficult for any leader to sustain and survive with his commitment in a country which is wedded to a new social order--democracy, secularism, and equality, that has not yet become an integral part of Indian culture, and where individual values are still pervasive in the lives of the millions of men. While confronted with these realities of life, whether the emerging leaders in rural India have a psychological predisposition to fight against the social inequalities with an integrity and commitment is the basic issue that calls for an empirical investigation.

In a transitional society, with the interaction of forces of modernization and traditionalism, it is essential to study the necessary and sufficient conditions of democratic functioning, the continuous in-flow of new social groups into leadership positions and their success in achieving equality, the new catchment areas of leadership. In the interaction between traditional social structure and modern democratic forms it would be worthwhile to enquire into the characteristics of such leaders.

With a view to examining the psychological pre-disposition of the rural leaders towards the complex process of democratization, the researcher identified the major variables involving a cluster of subtle Indian characteristics. Some of the studies undertaken in the area of rural leadership indicated that new patterns of talented leadership have been coming up with the introduction of community development and Panchayati Raj.

Based on the findings of those studies, in the area of rural leadership, one may notice the following trends in the pattern of emerging leadership.*

1. The sources of recruitment of new leaders are wider and not confined to traditionally entrenched land lords, village chiefs, and a few caste Hindu-families.[34]

2. The middle castes are also assuming leadership position in the basis of their numerical strength and their newly acquired wealth.[35]

3. Education, exposure to mass-media, secular orientation, social participation, innovations, political awareness, achievement motivation, and empathy are considered to be some of the new determinants of leadership.[36]

Though it is reported in many studies that there is emergence of new leadership associated with the introduction of community development and Panchayati Raj, it is observed that the traditional factors like caste[37] and economic position[38] still continue to be effective.

It is also to be noted in this context that most of the studies in India were confined to a single village or a group of villages, dealing with one or two aspects of leadership, and comparing those findings with that of the non-leaders. With few exceptions, little attention has been paid to study the degree of exposure to mass-media and extension agency contacts, the levels of aspirations, social awareness, and the attitude towards democratic vs. authoritarianism among the rural leaders, in the context of our social, political and economic changes.

Social scientists are concerned today with understanding and interpreting the various aspects of leadership pattern. With few exceptions little attention has been given to such studies of leadership in Andhra Pradesh which is equally exposed to economic, political, social and cultural changes.

However, leaders in the Indian villages are not necessarily formal leaders. Political affiliations, official positions and professional attainment may not be the characteristics of the most influential leaders in the rural community, but these are silently trusted, people consult them, seek their advice and listen to them with respect. They are invited to important ceremonies, called upon to settle disputes, and chosen to the place of responsibility. Their influence may or may not overflow the village boundaries, they may not be active in party politics, and some of them probably have never contested elections for any office, but still they are instrumental in process of decision making. They do not exercise power by themselves, but they control others who exercise powers. Oomen distinguishes these informal and formal leaders as power reservoirs and power exercisers.[39]

It is easy to identify formal leaders, who hold offices in formal organisations or elected to places of responsibility. But it is difficult to identify these socially influential informal leaders who hold no office and still enjoy considerable prestige, who are sought after for advice on various community affairs, and who can successfully ,gear community activities in definite directions. It is equally important to have an understanding of these informal leaders.

Therefore, in the present study, an attempt is made to understand the nature of the rural leaders, from socio-psychological point of view, in order to answer the following questions.

1. Which socio-economic background do the leaders emerge from?

2. To what extent the rural leaders are exposed to mass media and have contacts with extension agency?

3. What are the levels of their aspirations ?

4. Are these leaders aware of social, economic and political changes occurring in the community?

5. Are the rural leaders in general authoriarian or, democratic in their attitude ?

6. Is there any association between :

   (a) the socio-economic background and democratic vs. authoritarian behaviour of the rural leaders ?

(b) the degree of exposure to mass-media and extension agency contact and democratic vs. authoritarian behaviour of the rural leaders ?

(c) the levels of aspirations and democratic vs. authoritarian behaviour of rural leaders ?

(d) the level of social awareness and democratic vs. authoritarian behaviour of rural leaders ?

These are some of the questions raised in the study which give direction to the general framework of the investigation which covers:

1. The socio-economic status of the rural leaders and its influence on their democratic vs. authoritarian behaviour.

2. Influence of mass-media and contacts with extension agency on the democratic vs. authoritarian behaviour of rural leaders.

3. The relationship between the aspiration levels of the rural leaders and their democratic vs. authoritarian behaviour.

4. The levels of social awareness of the rural leaders in relation to their democratic vs. authoritarian behaviour.

Notes and References

1. David C. McClelland (1961),. *The Achieving Society*, (New York, D. Van Nostrand Company. INC), pp. 1-15.

2. The Biographies of leaders support this statement, Vidya Dhar Mahajan, (1975) *Leaders of the Nationalist Movement*, (New Delhi: Sterling Publishers Pvt.Ltd.)

3. Airan.J.W., "The Crisis of Leadership". In J.W. Airan, (ed) (1969). *The Nature of Leadership*, (Bombay: Lalvani Publishing House,) pp.1-2.

4. Gunnar Myrdal, "Soft State". In *The Challenge of World Poverty, A World Antipoverty Programme* (Australia, Penguin Books Australia Ltd. 1970), p.211.

5. Fairchild H.P. (1967). *Dictionary of Sociology* (Totawa: N.J. Littlefield Adms. and Co.,), p. 174.

6. Cecil A Gibb, "Leadership". In *International Encyclopedia of Social Sciences,* (ed), David L. Sills (New York. The Macmillan Co. & The Free Press, 1968) Vol.9, pp.90-101.
7. Ordway Tead (1963). *The Art of Leadership,* (New York: McGraw Hill Book Co.,).
8. Richard Schnridt; "Leadership". *Encyclopedia of Social Sciences,* (ed), Edwin R.A. Seligman, (1957), Vol. IX-X, p. 282.
9. Dube S.C., "A Frame Work for The Study of Rural Leadership in Transitional Societies". In *Emerging Patterns of Rural Leadership in Southern Asia,* ed. Leela Dube, (Hyderabad, National Institute of Community Development, 1965), p.24.
10. Murray G. Rose and Charles E. Hendry, (1957). *New Understanding of Leadership", A Survey and Application of Research,* (New York: Association Press,), p. 22.
11. Frankly Haiman, (1951). *Group Leadership and Democratic Action,* (Massachusetts, Houghton Mifflin Co.,), p.14.
12. Charles P. Loomis, "Change in Rural India as related to Social Power and Sex". In *Behavioural Sciences and Community Development,* (Hyderabad, National Institute of Community Development, March 1967, Vol.I.), p.4.
13. *Ibid.*
14. Charles P, Loomis and Z.K. Loomis (eds), (1969). *Socio-Economic Change and the Religion Factor in India: An Indian Symposium of Views on Max Weber,* (New Delhi, Affiliated East-West Press,) p. 63.
15. Daniel, Ingalls, "The Brahmin Tradition". In Singer, Milton (ed), (1959) *Traditional India: Structure and Change* (Philadelphia: American Folklore Society,).
16. Dr. (Smt.) Abida Samiuddin (1977). "The Emerging Pattern of Rural Leadership", *Kurukshetra,* (February,), p. 4.
17. Singer, Milton, (ed). *Traditional India: Structure and Change, op.cit.*
18. Karl W. Deutsch, "Social Mobilisation and Political Development", *American Political Science Review,* Vol. IV, No.3, (September, 1961), pp.493-94.
19. Pai Panandikar, "Development Administration—An Approach", *The Indian Journal of Public Administration,* Vol.X, No.1, (January-March, 1964), p. 34.
20. Uday Mehata, "The Impact of The Panchayat Raj on Rural India". In *Rural Sociology in India,* ed., A.R. Desai, 5th Edition (Bombay, Popular Publications, 1978), p. 591.
21. *Ibid,* p. 592.
22. Srinivas, M.N. (1962). *Caste in Modern India,* (Bombay: Asia Publishing House).

23. Sirsikar V.M. (1950). *The Rural Elite in a Developing Society*, (New Delhi: Orient Longmans, Ltd.).
24. *Ibid.*
25. Myrdal G., *Soft State: The Challenge of World Poverty—Anti Poverty Programme: an Outline, op.cit.*, pp. 211-212.
26. Sirsikar V.M., *op.cit.* p. 188.
27. Srivastava S.K., "Directed Social Change and Rural Leadership in India". In Leela Dube, ed. *Emerging Patterns of Rural Leadership in Southern Asia*, (Hyderabad : National Institute of Community Development, 1965),p.152.
28. Alex Inkles, "Making Men Modern: On the Causes and Consequences of Individual Change in Six Developing Countries". *American Journal of Sociology*, Vol.75, No. 2, (1969),p.210.
29. J. Filella, S.J., "The Psychology of Leadership". In *The Nature of Leadership—A Practical Approach*, (ed) J.W. Airan, (Bombay: Lalvani Publishing House, 1969), p. 60.
30. Thirtha N.V., "A Comparative Study of Gandhiji's Educational Ideas and the Government of India's Basic Education Programme—A Study in Values," Unpublished Ph.D. dissertation, Stanford University, 1959, pp.82-89.
31. Desai, A.R. (1976). *Rural Sociology in India*, (Bombay: Popular Prakashan,), p. 54.
32. Dube, S.C., "Modernization and Its Adaptive Demands on Indian Society". In M.S. Gore and others, (ed) (1967) *Papers in the Sociology of Education in India*, (Delhi: NCERT,).
33. Hiren J. Pandya, "Development Administration and Rural Leadership in India", *Social Change*, Vol.5, No.3 & 4, (September-December 1975), pp.20-21.
34. Singh, B.N., "The Impact of the Community Development Programme on Rural Leadership". In Park, R.L., and Tinker, Irene, ed., *Leadership and Political Institutions in India*, (Princeton University Press, 1959), pp. 358-71.
35. (i) Andre Beteille, "Caste old and new": *Essays in Social Structure and Social Stratification*, (Bombay: Asia Publishing House, 1969).
    (ii) *Caste, Class and Power: Changing Patterns of Stratification in a Tanjore Village*, (Bombay: Oxford University Press, 1966).
36. (i) Abraham M. Francis, (1974). *Dynamics of Leadership in Village India*, (Allahabad: Indian International Publication).
    (ii) Singh M.P. and Mishra R.P., "Characteristics of the Emerging Village Leaders", *Interdiscipline*, Vol.10,No.2, (Summer, 1973), pp.93-106.
37. (i) Sirsikar, V.M., *The Rural Elite in a Developing Society, op.cit.*
    (ii) Ram Reddy, G., and Seshadri K. (1972). *The Voter and Panchayat Raj—A Study of the Electoral Behaviour during Panchayat Elections in Warangal,*

District, Andhra Pradesh, (Hyderabad), (National Institute of Community Development,).

(iii) Bada, C.R. (1975). "Village Panchayat Key Leadership Pattern", *Interdiscipline,* Vol.12, No.2, pp. 71-82.

38. (i) Mehata, S.R., (1972). *Emerging Pattern of Rural Leadership* (Bombay: Wiley Eastern).

(ii) Sirsikar, V.M., *The Rural Elite in a Developing Soceity, op.cit.*

39. Oomen, T.K. (1970). "Rural Community Power Structure in India", *Social Forces,* 49 (2), pp.226-239.

2

AN OVERVIEW OF THE EXISTING LITERATURE

Most of the new nations of the world are committed to a policy of planned economic and social change. In many of them the process of modernisation is being pressed at an accelerated pace. In reference to these countries the study of the existing and the emerging patterns of leadership has assumed a crucial significance.

Studies on patterns and processes of rural leadership represent a comparatively new interest in social science researches.

Generally it is observed that the leadership phenomenon is contextual in nature, and the context in the case of India, especially with regard to rural leadership, is constituted of socio-economic, and to some extent political conditions. Until recently, this context was almost wholly characterized by caste, family and kinship loyalties and ascriptive status. This being so, the sources of leadership recruitment were few, closed and predetermined. The functions forming the role of this leadership were generally diffused and oriented towards maintaining the status-quo rather than towards achievements.

Recent research inquiries indicate[1] that the Indian rural communities are changing, and in this process of planned socio-economic change, considerable trasformation has been brought about in the context of the leadership. This has raised the interest of social scientists towards studying the leadership pattern.

During the last few years some field research has been done in the area of rural leadership in India. In this chapter, an attempt is made to briefly review the available studies on different aspects of leadership.

Abraham[2] while reviewing the studies on leadership in rural India, has classified them into two phases. Basing on the mode of inquiry, selection of variables and the radius of their explanatory-shell, these studies have been classified into conventional and progressive phases. These phases do not represent two chronological sequences and they are not classified as earlier and recent studies in leadership.

According to Abraham the studies in the conventional phase are concerned with dynamics of leadership, as evidenced in village factions, economic status, caste hierarchy, and family prestige. Their universe is self-contained communities, their autonomous cultural systems, the restricted spheres of social influence confined to narrowly defined social networks and extended kinship ties. Their criteria of leadership are conventional and the characteristics they have unearthed are largely traditional. Social change served as a remote background to, rather than an integral part of, leadership studies.[3]

Studies on leadership in the progressive phase have taken the processes and dynamics of modernisation into consideration. They have dealt with actual as well as potential challenges to traditional authority and documented the emergence of new patterns of leadership. Their universe is the changing rural communities caught up in the mainstream of national progress. These studies have evolved some modern criteria of leadership based on the changes and challenges perpetuated by the forces of modernization.[4]

Dhillon, Epstein, Majumdar, Lewis, Mandelbaum, Ranga Rao, Harijindar Singh and many others have explained traditional leadership in terms of characteristics unique to Indian rural social system. Position in the local caste hierarchy, wealth reputation and size of the family, age, connections and influene outside the village, knowledge of court affairs, hospitality and elaborate performance of the ceremonies are considered the most important attributes of leadership in villages of India.[5] Prodipto Roy, Lalit K. Sen, Fliegel, Vidyarthi, Loomis, Narain, Bhat Kumar, Abraham and others have in their efforts to highlight leadership in the progressive phase, ascribed high predictive validity of several modern variables. some of the new determinants of leadership so unearthed are education, literacy, exposure to mass media, cosmopoliteness, social participation, innovativeness, secular orientation, political knowledge, ability, motivation and empathy.[6]

However, coming to the principal findings or various studies, one can notice that the studies of rural leadership in India have started in the anthropological tradition. Lewis and Dhillon initiated full length studies of factions and leadership in North and South Indian villages respectively. These studies have dealt with the varied roles of caste and kinship factions in the decision-making process in rural India.

Oscar Lewis[7] has studied the dynamics of rural leadership. He has analysed the nature and functions of 'factions' in a Jat village near Delhi. He pointed out how patterns of influence and communication within extended family groups reach out to several villages. Jat factions as described by him, are based on kinship.[8] In his study of "Village life in Northern India" he has touched on the dynamics of rural leadership.[9] He concluded "An analysis of the personal and socio-economic characteristics of Jat leaders reveals that, leadership depends upon the following factors in order of importance : wealth, family reputation, age and genealogical position, personality traits, education, connections and influence with outsiders and finally numerical strength of the family and lineages.[10]

Lewis's study brought out significant correlation between leadership and family size.[11] A positive relationship has been identified, between family income and leadership. According to Lewis "wealth is a basic criterion for leadership. Although leaders are found among all three socio-economic classes, they clearly come from the upper levels of each and the correlation between wealth and leadership is the highest as we move up the scale."[12]

Dhillon has studied leadership and Groups in a south Indian village. His technique of identifying village leaders is "to observe their leadership roles. Occasions like court quarrels, meetings of Panchayat held, to settle important disputes or to settle arrangements for village wide festivals and ceremonies like marriages are the important ones which reveal who are the most important and influential persons in the village. The information obtained by this indirect method is supplemented and checked by direct questioning of the selected respondents. Each respondent is asked to name the persons who, take an active interest in village affairs, are invited to attend Panchayat meetings and are honoured during ceremonies and festivals."[13]

Dhillon, in terms of prominence or importance, has classified leaders into 'primary', 'secondary', and 'tertiary' leaders. Primary or major leaders, are those whose presence is considered essential in all important meetings of the village Panchayat, held for any purpose. Secondary leaders are those who have occupied important positions in their respective factions. Tertiary or minor leaders are those who represent small kinship units of four or five families.[14]

According to Dhillon, factors contributing to leadership can be classified into three categories:[15] social status of the family, inherited social position and reputation of the family, size of the family, elaborate performance of ritualistic ceremonies, and wealth, contribute to leadership. Other factors that improve leadership chances are age, leisure time available, inclination to attend social and ceremonial matters, hospitality, influence outside the village either through marital relations with important families or contacts with officials, knowledge of court affairs and education.[16] On the attributes of rural leadership Lewis and Dhillon have reached strikingly similar conclusions. Dhillon like Lewis also pointed out a positive relationship between family income and leadership. Dhillon reprots, "wealth is one of the most important criteria for leadership. Some of the persons who are not from families with inherited claims to Yajamanship have attained leadership status by virtue of their wealth which has generally been acquired in trade."[17]

However, these studies do not adequately cover the dynamism and mobility pattern among leaders. But these studies on the power structure in rural India inspired a number of scholars from various parts of the world to begin the study of rural leadership in different parts of India.

A major attempt in the study of rural leadership came with the publication of the edited volume of Park and Tinker[18] which includes a number of papers on the various aspects of leadership in rural India.

Evelyn Wood[19] his study of reviewed some of the published studies on leadership in rural India and discussed the changes in the pattern of leadership. He has pointed out several types of leaders, such as the aristrocrat, the religious, professional, the oligarch, the bureaucrat, and the family or faction autocrat.[20]

He has also discussed about some of the intermediary channels of influence. He has pointed out that in the leadership structure of rural India, one factor is common to the whole countryside: "A would-be or putative leader, who offers counsel or who gives orders calling for a new practice or a changed practice on the part of his fellow villagers, will not be taken seriously, for long unless he himself and his family, follow consistently the changes required."[21]

Baji Nath Singh, in his study, has identified the emergence of a new and young leadership. According to him, the transformation is the consequence of land reforms, education and democratization. The leadership emerging as consequence of concentrated developmental activity, has certain characteristic features. He found that the new leaders belonged to the middle or younger age group. This new leadership, as he observes are adequatedly interested in community development projects. The sources of recruitment of the new leadership are also wider, not confined to traditionally entrenched landlord, village chief and a few caste Hindu families. The rich families who had been influential in the past, lost their influence because of their lack of interest in community welfare programmes and because of various legislative and political changes. From autocratic or authoritarian leadership has become democratic.[22]

According to Baji Nath Singh, there is a growing awareness and desire among many members of the community to take leadership roles and to devote time to community activities. The community developmental activities by providing opportunities to more dynamic individuals to work for the community, help to make the new leadership an integral part of the democratic process.[23]

Like Wood, John Hitchcock[24] in his study of leadership in a north Indian village, has held that caste as a basis of leadership has been continuing, though among lower caste there is growing consciousness of the need for economic reform.

Further he finds that the caste leaders to be more educated and development oriented.[25]

Henry Orenstein's study persents aspects of leadership behaviour in a village in Poona district. He has examined both 'formal' and 'informal' leaders. Informal leaders are further classified into 'sanctioned' and 'unsanctioned' types.[26] The author has observed that though persons of high repute and status are elected to formal positions in the newly established Panchayats, they tend to embody the functional roles more in their personal capacity than make efforts to institutionalize it.[27]

Alan Beals[28] in his study of Mysore village has found that while traditional leadership is losing its influence, no clear trends about the new leadership are noticeable. He has suggested that the implication of factionalism for village-wide leadership is that there can be no village-wide leadership.[29] McCormack has identified three reasons for the decline of the power of traditional leadership. They are:

1. secularization of the villagers' outlook,

2. the questioning of the neutrality and good character of some of the village elders, and

3. the waning interest on the part of important village leaders in their traditional role of arbitrators of village disputes.[30]

He concludes that the village life has undergone two significant changes which seems to be responsible for the growing importance of factional leadership. The first is the change in the pattern of village economy, i.e. from an economy based on subsistence farming characterized by free and voluntary exchange of labour among farming families the village has shifted, to an economy in which cash farming with hired labour and outside employment form an important part. The second change is the increase in the extent of direct governmental interference in village affairs, which has influenced the growth of factionalism in the village.[31]

Bachenheimer's[32] study is mainly concerned with studying the roles of village leaders. He has observed that wealth and high caste determine the shape of village leadership and within each caste the most important attribute of leadership is economic status. Thus real power is wielded by a few outward looking families with economic and party interests beyond the village. Education is considered a valued asset for leadership. In spite of wider orientation, the pattern of leadership is traditional. The lower caste leader who serves as a channel of communication between the village leaders and the lower castes are allowed to exist porvided they know their place. According to him with an increase in literacy, and improvement in the general level of education and in communication media there would be an increase in political awareness and the villager would become more prone to participate in political acitivity.[33]

Harper and Edward[34] in their study have observed that on the whole the village retains its traditional fòrms of leadership, decision making, and censure. Major leadership roles are filled by the Havik brahmins and the political dynamics of feud, friendship, faction, and party play an important part in determining which individual will attain these positions.

Srinivas and Dube have made specific contribution to the study of leadership both in terms of concepts and methods. Srinivas[35] regards the concept of "dominant caste" as crucial for the study of leadership. He observes that he dominant caste is functional for the maintenance of village community and also works as a reference point for the lower castes to improve their position, both social and economic.

According to him in understanding a village, it is essential to study the locally dominant caste and the kind of dominance it wields. He has identified four important elements of dominance:

(1) Numerical strength;

(2) Economic and political power;

(3) Ritual status; and

(4) Western education and occupations.[36]

According to him these elements are distributed among different castes in a village ana only the caste enjoying all or most of them can have decisive dominance.[37] On the other hand, Dube[38] feels that the concept of dominant caste is not of much help, since only a handful of individuals or families in a caste hold the prestige of status symbols, financial resources, and positions of influence within and outside the caste group. Some other investigators' findings also have not supported Srinivas's thesis.

Wiser and Wiser in their study have observed that "if caste precedence and economic power rest in the same men their leadership is assured. If the two qualities are separate, villages follow the man who can grant or withhold their daily bread. Ordinarily we find this power resting with the twice born."[39]

In the proceedings[40] of "International Round Table Conference on Emerging Patterns of Rural Leadership in South Asia", papers of Dube and Leela Dube, on methodological problems and a survey of contemporary literature on the subject, and papers on the results of similar studies undertaken in Pakistan, Ceylon, Indonesia etc., have been included. Rajni Kothari does the summing up in which he has presented the emerging trends against a cross cultural comparative persDective. These papers have covered structural, functional and behavioural aspects of emerging rural leadership.

Another sutdy of emerging leadership in rural India has resulted from a seminar held at Ranchi University.[41] The papers dealing with the leadership pattern in Uttar Pradesh, Bihar, Rajasthan and Punjab are important in this regard. According to these studies the role of traditional factors is on the decline, but money still remains as the most important bases of leadership. To some extent education is also believed to be playing a vital role in the make-up of leaders.[42]

Most of these studies overemphasized the attributes of rural leadership in terms of ascription and achievement and discussed the nature of leadership in terms of formal and informal and faction-oriented and unified leadership patterns. These are not studies of rural leadership in all its aspects. Not much light is thrown on the leaders' stand as modernizing agents, their attitudes and values, how they communicate, behave and function and their perception of changes in the society.

Later a growing interest among social scientists, towards studying the emerging pattern of rural leadership in the context of India's modernization has been observed. Several studies have attempted to investigate the changes that have been brought about in the leadership pattern after the introduction of community development and Panchayati Raj.

These studies have observed that the new social and economic forces generated by the large scale development plans and attitude of the people in general and leaders are no exception to this.

Nagpaul observes, that the traditional leadership is also undergoing a change and new patterns of leadership are emerging on the scene. In this context, the introduction of community project, land reforms, decentralized local administration and adult franchise which aim at the reconstruction of rural society, have brought forth the importance of leadership.[43]

Prodipto Roy in his study has analyzed the characteristics of emergent leaders and comes to the following conclusions.

(1) Individuals with a high income and high level of living are likely to become leaders in the new organization of the village.

(2) Members with large families are likely to emerge as leaders.

(3) Level of education of the members determines the level of the leaders in these social organization.

(4) Age, and caste are not considered determining factors of leadership.

(5) The new leaders are seemed to have a higher level of contact with village people.[44]

In another study[45] it is observed that urban contacts, high economic and family status, personal qualities useful to influence people, participation in community activities and formal education are associated with the emergence of leadership.

Andre Beteille studied distribution of social power in a Tanjore village.[46] He has observed that up to 1940s the power in the village was based on conventional factors like ownership of land, high social and ritual stutus and superior education. Brahmins dominated the system of social stratification and enjoyed an almost exclusive monopoly of conventional resources of power.[47] But all this began to change gradually. With the technological revolution in agriculture and land reforms, the middle castes are also assuming leadership positions on the basis of their numerical strength and their newly acquired wealth. Numerical strength emerged as a decisive determinant of leadership and the inherited social status was relegated to the background. In fact, the new peasant proprietor class now wields political influence.[48] Further he holds that lower castes will not acquire a position in the elite group until the agrarian structure is thoroughly transformed.[49]

Ranga Rao's study of an Andhra village reveals that the village is dominated by primary leaders, though a gradual growth of multiple secondary leadership is in the offing.[50] He observes that the introduction of Panchayati Raj elections led to the concentration of leadership in the numerically and economically important caste groups. His findings have supported the Srinivas's theory of 'Dominant Caste'.[51]

While studying the socio-economic characteristics of elected Panchayati Raj leaders in Orissa, Rout[52] has observed that the majority of them are from high castes, hig income group, agricultural and business professions. Similar conclusions have arrived with regard to the caste and economic background of the leaders by Pande and Jain[53] and Nair[54].

Some studies have been carried out by National Institute of Community Development for the review of Panchayat Raj as operating in Andhra Pradesh, Rajasthan, Gujarat, Maharashtra, and Tamil Nadu.[55]

The Maharashtra study explains that talented leadership is coming up and the democratic functioning of Panchayati Raj institutions depends upon the calibre of rural leadership. According to this study the leadership appears to be concerned with expectations for community welfare and shows awareness of the need for community social change. The findings of the Gujarat study are similar to that of Maharashtra study. This study has noted the emergence of leaders from the landed classes. The Rajasthan study provides a different picture. It is observed that though comparatively young and better educated leadership is in the offing, caste, in terms of rank and strength, family status and economic position continue to be its effective basis. In Andhra, the leadership is not progressive in outlook, though it has taken keener interest in developmental activities. All these studies bring out two common trends, first, comparatively speaking, the new leadership emerging in the wake of Panchayati Raj is less tradition-oreinted than the vast majority of their fellow-citizens in rural India, and second: political linkages and party affiliation are not well established at the village level.[56]

According to S.C.Jain's study[57] people with little education are elected to various offices under Panchayati Raj. It is noticed that Panchayati Raj organizations have been captured by unprogressive and irresponsible leaders. A big chasm is noticed between the leaders and led. Further the middle class leadership (such as lawyers, doctors, trade unionists) which could provide necessary mobility without jeopardising the stability, is conspicuously absent.

In the study of the "Emerging Pattern of Leadership in Panchayat Raj set-up in Mysore State", Bhat has observed that besides the variables like contacts with banks, proficiency in languages and political affiliations are also significantly related to leadership. According to Bhat, though there is no sudden change in the emerging pattern of rural leadership the gradual transformation to modernity is remarkably clear.[58] His study points to the emergence of young better educated leaders, as well as to the increasing involvement of Scheduled Castes in successive elections. The hold of upper strata in terms of both caste and class is said to be persisting. He has also pointed out that progressive sections of the rural community are acquiring leadership positions in Panchayati Raj bodies.[59]

Sen and Roy in their study have compared the characteristics of leaders and non-leaders and observed that the percentage of leaders' scores at about every positive score point on all aspects is higher than that of the non-leaders. The percentage of leaders reading newspapers is higher than that of the non-leaders. The urban links of leaders is higher than that of the non-leaders. On the sacred secular scale, the scores of leaders consistently fell towards the secular end of the continuum. Their study has revealed that the leaders are Brahmins or high caste non-Brahmins, and they are better educated and possess high economic status than the non-leaders.[60]

Another study has revealed that the leaders are more scientific, less tradition-oreinted and hold higher value for task-oriented behaviour than non-leaders.[61]

Fliegel and others studied the relationship between the selected characteristics of leaders and village-level adoption of agricultural innovations. The researchers argue: "Caste positions of leaders play an important role in village modernization. As a bridge between the traditional past and the new, caste still guarantees a higher social status to the leaders, which helps them to be modern (high extension agency contact, high urban contact, secular orientation and credit risk orientation) and to influence the whole village in that direction. Some of the so-called modern characteristics, such as empathy, and favourable opinion of extension programmes are found to be dependent on the caste status."[62]

Sen has undertaken the most thorough going study on opinion leadership in India. The major findings of Sen's study on opinion leadership may be summarized as follows.

(1) Leaders have, a higher caste status and higher level of living than non-leaders.

(2) Leaders are much more in touch with the outside world through visits to urban centres, education, political knowledge ability, exposure to mass media and contact with extension agency than non-leaders.

(3) They have more progressive outlook than non-leaders.

(4) Leaders in India dominate not only the political life of the village but other walks of life as well. In the Indian villages, it is observed that the formal leadership and opinion leadership considerably overlap.[63]

Singh and Mishra[64] have studied the characteristics of the emerging, traditional and formal leaders, in respect of their certain socio-psycho-personal variables. The study has revealed that emerging and the informal leaders are homogeneous in respect of their socio-economic status, caste, occupation, outside contacts and sacred secular predisposition. But they differ in respect of their age, and educational background. It is further observed that the emerging leaders are young in age, and relatively have more, outside contacts, education, secular pre-disposition than traditional leaders. But they do not differ with respect to their socio-economic status, caste. It is clear thast the socio-economic status and the caste of the individuals are determining factors in making them as leaders.

Abraham's study reveals that farm size, extension agency contact, newspaper exposure, social participation, secular orientation, and empathy are the important variables which explain the variance in community leadership. On the other hand, age, farm size, social participation and innovativeness have turned out to be the major determinants of agricultural opinion leadership.[65]

Abraham observes that, most of the characteristics ordinarily associated with leasdership in village India, namely, age, caste-rank, farm size, education, extension agency contact, newspaper exposure, cosmopoliteness and political abilities are still relevant one way or the other. However, they lack predictive validity and fail to explain leadership adequately when the influence of other variables is parcelled out.[66]

Abraham has classified leaders into two categories. The potential leader and the dynamic leader. A potential leader is one who has access to the sources of power and who possesses those characteristics which are traditionally associated with leadership. A dynamic leader is one who actually exercises power and is nominated to place of responsibility by other actors in the social system. The very fact that social participation is the most significant correlate of leadership implies that people tend to choose as their leaders those individuals who are actively involved in the affairs of the community rather than those who possess all the paraphernalia of leadership but are only passive spectators of on-going community activities.[67]

Abraham has explained this phenomenon as the theory of structural devalution of power. The theory postulates that in modernizing village India there is a gradual transfer of power from potential leaders to dynamic leaders from those who only own the conventional resources of power to those who also dominate fuctional spheres of the community.

This theory is futher supported by the fact that the most significant correlates of community leadership are measures of systemic linkage-extension agency contact, newspaper exposure, and social participation. Abraham also hypothesizes that the process of structural devolution of community power varies directly with the process of modernization. That is, as the pace and degree of modernization increase, more and more power is devolved and delegated to active community influentials.[68]

Abraham futher has observed the behavioural differences and differences of value orientations of opinion leaders and community leaders.

Sirsikar, in his article, "Leadership Pattern in Rural Maharashtra", has focused his attention on the socio-economic background, educational attainments, political experience, and role perception of rural leaders. One of the significant points made in this paper is that leaders are elected on a party ticket by secret ballot and as per the procedure laid down. But at the same time traditional factors such as kinship and caste are in evidence and the party structure itself is threatened with infiltration by these traditional elements.[69]

In another paper, he points out that the emerging leadership is in the process of closing the gap between the westernised elites and the masses. he observes that the new rural leaders have been found to be mass-oriented, and 'verbally committed' to the new ideas of economic development, universal education, social equality and democratic politics.[70]

Sirsikar has also made full length study of rural leadership. The major concern of the study was to explore "the hitherto unexplored areas of political socialization, recruitment, value orientations and psychological perception of the leaders."[71] With this purpose in view, the study has tried to bring to light:

(1) the socio-economic and political career background of the leader,

(2) leaders' perception of community problems,

(3) leaders' innovative capacity,

(4) leaders' attitudes, motivations, and values,

(5) leaders' opinion on the functioning of the Panchayati Raj,

(6) leaders' awareness and acceptance of the national goals.

Some of the major findings of this study are:

(1) the leaders come from the richer peasantry which has tradition, social status, wealth and other factors on its side,

(2) the gap between the leader and the led is very wide,

(3) there is a trend towards concentration of socio-economic and political power,

(4) the leadership situation is characterised by the "tribe monopoly of class, the peasantry, a caste, Maratha, and a party—the Congress",

(5) the rural leaders had by and large, strong linkages with political leadership at higher levels,

(6) politics of patronage and bargaining has replaced the politics of service and sacrifice. The study also reveals that a discernible power orientation.[72]

Iqbal Narain[73] has examined the qualitative changes in panchayat leadership in respect of two phases. The significant points made by this study are:

Phase-I[74]

(1) There was a balance between service-cum-development mechanisms.

(2) There was an acceptance of non-traditional traits among the leaders.

(3) The old traditional leaders have retained position albeit under changed conditions and with apparently different attitudes.

(4) Political parties were, by and large, absent from the scene and the caste, family status were dominant factors.

(5) Age, education and occupation did not play any important role.

Phase-II[75]

(1) Operation of political parties penetrated these institutions.

(2) Service-and-development orientation was replaced by power-orientation, and consequently the control over distribution of scarce goods and services assumed crucial importance for leadership.

This survey of the studies of Sirsikar and Iqbal Narain has been summed up in the words of Ram Reddy and Seshadri, thus: "While Sirsikar's study emphasized the role of traditional social structure in politics and Iqbal Narain's study highlights the transformation brought about by politics, both aspects seem to be two aspects of the same leadership dynamics in which politics play an increasing role".

Harjinder Singh's[76] study is an attempt to study the leadership pattern based on influence and authority, and to examine the various characteristics of leaders as compared with non-leaders. The major findings of the study are:-

(a) The formal leadership structure is highly specialized.

(b) The formal leaders tend to be influential in community issues.

(c) Informal structure is more powerful in generating influential than the formal structure. The formal structure is open for men and women, whereas the informal influence structure is not open to female participation as influentials in community issues.[77]

The characteristics, attitudes and beliefs of the leaders are compared with that of the non-leaders. It is found that the leaders as compared to non-leaders generally belong to upper caste, higher social class, higher income group and they own more land. He further observes that the opinion sentiments towards various referents are more favourable among leaders than non-leaders. Their reactions to various hypothetical action situations are more positive as against non-leaders. The attitude and behaviour of leaders towards various referents are more positive and favourable in comparison to the non-leaders. Leaders as compared to non-leaders are found to be with less tradition orientations, high value standards, stronger group expectations, self-commitment, more ability to do various jobs, more group support in participation in various activities. The leaders tend to be more change-oriented than non-leaders.[78]

Saran[79] has attempted to study the pattern of leadership in the context of modernization of our country. The main purpose of this study is to explore the extent to which changes in the economic, political and social conditions in a modernising society such as India result in corresponding changes in the attitudes and values of rural leadership.

With this purpose in view the study has tried to bring to light:

(a) the profiles of leaders in the context to the changing socio-political scene of India,

(b) attitudes of the leaders towards new panchayats, land reforms, and developmental plans,

(c) the relation between economic, political and social conditions of modernizing country and the attitudes and value of rural leadership.[80]

The study has revealed that the leaders are also emerging from younger age group. Leadership is distributed among the upper, intermediate, and lower castes of the village and it is not concentrated among the upper caste alone. Land, money and land ownership are important factors of leadership positions. The educational level is strikingly high. In terms of mass media exposure and outside contacts, the leaders have high exposure to mass media and have greater contacts with outside agencies. Affiliation to formal organizations like political, vocational, and professional is low.[81]

He has studied further the relationship between economic, political and social conditions of the village and the attitudes and the values of the leaders. On the basis of the findings it is concluded that the economic, political and social conditions in a modernizing society do affect the attitudes and values of rural leadership. But the effect is not so inclusive and traditionalism is replaced by modernity. It is observed that modernisation did not proceed in a unidimensional direction. Rural leaders are modern in one sphere and traditional in another. Though in some instances, a dichotomy is noticed, a continuum between tradition and modernity is also noticed.[82]

There are number of other studies, most of them in the form of papers published in journals or in edited works, either having total focus on rural leadership or dealing with some of the dimensions of leadership pattern.

The major findings yielded by the reserch studies may be summed up as follows.

(1) A new rural leadership emerging from the higher income group and more educated sections of the rural society is dominating Panchayati Raj institutions to-day.

(2) The new leadership is younger in age, better educated, has better economic status and the dominant caste is better represented in panchayats.

(3) The Panchayati Raj organisation is captured by "unprogressive and irresponsible leadership". The leadership is dominated by the former landed interests, merchants and traditionalists. There is a big gap between the leader and the led.

(4) No significant correlation is noticed between socio-economic status and the key leadership pattern in village panchayat institution.

(5) The new leadership has shown more interest in the exercise of power than the inclination to shoulder the responsibility.

(6) A trend towards concertration of socio-economic and political power is discernible.

(7) There is a need to foster new sources of leadership from the peasants and artisan castes so as to break the iron strangle-hold which landlords have on village life.

(8) The traditional leadership is usually associated with agricultural community and diversified occupations with newer and more modern leadership.

(9) Benefits of the government measures have reached villages through landlord repesentatives and officials who share the same socio-economic and educational background and this has led to the reinforcement of traditional authority.

(10) Intelligence, adjustment, dominance, self-confidence, extro-version, empathy, social perception and emotional stability are the qualities present among leaders to a greater extent in a variety of situations.

(11) Factionalism is an inherent part of the leadership situation in the villages in India, and due to economic change and government intervention, the traditional leader, though still exercising some force, is being challenged by new forces.

(12) Conflict and tension have arisen as a result of interaction between the power climbers and the traditional power holders.

(13) There is a gradual transformation of leadership in village India. It is gradually passing on to the younger elements with successive elections. Though the traditional leaders still have some control over the sources of power, their hold is loosening with successive elections.

(14) The present day leaders are giving up traditional way of life in perference to western and modern practices.

(15) The Panchayati Raj and Community Development Schemes have only helped powerful groups to make a further improvement in their own positions.

(16) It is only where better educated and comparatively young leadership is emerging that there an ideological orientation may be discerned.

(17) Emerging leaders compared to traditional leaders are found to be younger in age, have relatively more favourable attitudes towards new organisations, greater secular predisposition, more outside contacts and more education. But they do not differ with respect to socio-economic status, occupation and caste.

(18) The emerging leadership has shown relatively more secular orientation to life.

(19) A gradual transformation of leadership to modernity is 'remarkably clear'.

(20) Panchayat leaders by and large have a positive and progressive aspiration as required in the development administration, hence they can be viewed as change agents.

In the above summing up of the findings of the research studies, one point emerges clear that quite a few findings have certain common points to make. However, at the same time in certain findings on some vital points like the loosening of the hold of traditional leadership and its being passed on to the younger generation, there is a divergence of view. Some studies have come to the conclusion that the old traditional leadership is still persistent without there being any hope of replacing it by younger and newer kind of leadership in the near future. Some others have come to a definite conclusion that thrugh the old leadership still wields some power, it is in the process of being replaced by a more educated, younger and relatively modern and flexible leadership.

However, an overall observation on this aspect of rural leadership in India, has brought out the fact that the established position of traditional leaders is now on the decline, although in cases they continue to exert their influence in the community. Various socio-economic and political changes have affected their leadership and as a result some change is also noticed in the bases of leadership and methods or strategies of exercising power. All these observations are significant for any new investigation.

It is observed that in most of these studies attention is paid to study the personal, social and economic characteristics of leaders their value-orientations, attitudes, aspirations and behavioural patterns in general and in comparison with non-leaders. Further as the review shows very few studies have attempted to study the leaders' behaviour in terms of democratic vs. authoritarian behaviour.

There are wide array of social and personal characteristics which are associated with the behavioural patterns of the individuals. Little attention is paid to study the relationship between social and personal characteristics of leaders and their democratic vs. authoritarian behaviour. Further, it appears reasonable to suppose that characteristics found to be associated with leaders' behavioural pattern in one population may not show the same degree and direction of association in another population. In view of this it was felt that there is a need for a number of investigations, dealing with different sets of variables relevant for the local conditions. The present investigation has been conceived and carried out against this background.

Notes and References

1. Ishawaran, K. (ed.), (1970). *Change and Continuity in India's Villages*, (Columbia University Press,).
2. Abraham, M.P., "Studies in Leadership: A Critique on Empirical and Conceptual Analyses", *The Indian Journal of Social Work*, Vol. XXXIII, No.3, (October, 1972), pp.221-34.
3. *Ibid.*
4. *Ibid.*
5. *Ibid.*
6. *Ibid.*
7. Lewis Oscar, *Group Dynamics in a North Indian Village*, (Delhi: Planning commission, 1954).
8. *Ibid.*
9. Lewis Oscar, (1958). *Village Life in Northern India*, (Urbana University of Illinois Press,). p.127.
10. *Ibid.* pp. 129-30.
11. *Ibid.*
12. *Ibid.* p.16.
13. Dhillon H.S., (1955). "Leadership and Groups in a South Indian Village," (New Delhi. Planning Commission, PEO Publication No.9), p.12

14. *Ibid.* pp.115-16.
15. *Ibid.*
16. *Ibid*, pp.118-24.
17. *Ibid*, p.120.
18. Richard, L. Park and Irene Tinker (ed.), (1959). *Leadership and Political Institutions in India*, (Princeton N.J. Princeton University Press).
19. Wood, Evelyn, "Patterns of Influence within Rural India." In Park and Tinker (ed), *op.cit.*, pp. 372-90.
20. *Ibid.*
21. *Ibid.*
22. Singh, B.N., "the impact of the Community development Programme on Rural Leadership". In Park and Tinker (ed), *Ibid*, pp. 358-71.
23. *Ibid.*
24. Hitchcock, John T., "Leadership in a North Indian Village". In *Ibid*, pp.395-414.
25. *Ibid.*
26. Orenstein, Henry, "A Bombay Village". In *Ibid*, pp. 414-26.
27. *Ibid.*
28. Beals, Alan, "Leadership in a Mysore village". In *Ibid*, pp. 426-37.
29. *Ibid.*
30. McCormack, William, "Factionalism in a Mysore Village". In *Ibid*, pp.438-44.
31. *Ibid.*
32. Bachenbeimer, "Elements of Leadership in an andhra Village". In *Ibid*, pp.445-52.
33. *Ibid.*
34. Harper, Edward., and Loise G. Harper, "Political Organization and Leadership in a Karnataka Village". In *Ibid*, pp.453-69.
35. Srinivas, M.N., (1969). "The Dominant Caste in Rampura". In *American Anthropologist*, Vol. 61(1), February, pp.1-16.
36. *Ibid.*
37. *Ibid.*
38. Dube, S.C., "Caste Dominance and Factionalism" *Contributions to Indian Sociology*, New Series No.II, (December, 1968), pp.58-81.
39. Wiser, W.H. and Wiser C.N., (1964). *Behind Mud Walls 1930-60*, (Berkeley: University of California Press), pp.18-19.
40. Dube, S.C., (ed.). *Emerging Pattern of Rural Leadership in Southern Asia*, (Hyderabad: National Institute of Community Development,).
41. Vidyarthi, L.P., (ed.), (1967). *Leadership in India*, (Bombay: Asia Publishing House,).
42. *Ibid.*
43. Nagpal, in *Ibid*, p.58.
44. Prodipto Roy, in *Ibid*, p.224.
45. Salvi P.V. and Patil., R.Y., "Rural Local Leadership", *Rural India*, 31, No.9, (November, 1968), pp.343-45.

46. Beteille, Andre, *Caste, Class, and Power*, (Bombay. Oxford University Press, 1966).

47. *Ibid.*

48. *Ibid.*

49. *Ibid.*

50. Rao K. Ranga, "Leadership in a Community Development Village". In M.V. Moorthy (ed.), *Sociological Aspects of Community Development*, (Waltair, Andhra University 1966).

51. *Ibid.*

52. Rout, B., "Rural Leadership Problems". *Kurukshetra* 15, No.5 (February, 1967), pp.15-16.

53. Pande, B.M. and Jain P.N., "Rural Leadership Differentials in Emerging Pattern", *Kurukshetra*, 14 No.4. (January, 1966), pp.13-14.

54. Nair, S.P., "Leadership in Kerala Panchayats", *Khadi-gramodyog*, B, No.10, (July, 1967), pp.689-93.

55. Jacob George (ed.), (1971). *Readings on Panchayati Raj*, (Hyderabad: N.I.C.D.,).

56. *Ibid.*

57. Jain, S.C., (1967). *Community Development and Panchayati Raj in India*, (Delhi: Allied Publishers,), pp.611-27.

58. Bhat, K.S., "*Emerging Patterns of Leadership in Mysore State*", Jacob, George (ed.), *op.cit.*, pp.121-44.

59. *Ibid.*

60. Sen. Lalit. K. and Prodipto Roy. *Awareness of Community Develooment in village India*, (Hedrabad. N.I.C.D. 1967).

61. Singh, S.N. and Arya, H.P., "Value Orientations of Local Village Leaders", *Studies in Rural Leadership* (ed.), Udai Pareek, (Delhi. Behavioural Sciences Centre,) pp.23-30.

62. Fliegel, Frearick C., *et.al.* (1968). *Agricultural Innovations in Indian Villages*, (Hyderabad. N.I.C.D.). P.85.

63. Sen Lalit K., (1969) *Opinion Leadership in India*, (Hyderabad. N.I.C.D.), p.56.

64. Singh M.P. and Mishra R.P., "Characteristics of the Emerging Village Leaders", *Interdiscipline*, Vol.10, No.2 (Summer 1973).

65. Abraham, M.F., (1974). *The Dynamics of Leadership in Village India*, (Indian International Publications, Allahabad,).

66. *Ibid.*

67. *Ibid.*

68. *Ibid.*

69. Sirsikar V.M., "Leadership Pattern in Rural Maharashtra", *Asian Survey*, 4, (1964), pp.929-39.

70. Sirsikar V.M., "Political Role of Panchayati Raj", *Economic and Political Weekly*, Vol.I, No.14, (November 19, 1966), pp.581-84.

71. Sirsikar, V.M. *The Rural Elite in a Developing Society*, (Bombay, Orient Longman, 1970).

72. *Ibid.*

73. Iqbal Narain, "Democratic Decentralisation and Rural Leadership in India: Rajasthan Experiment", *Asian Survey*, , (August, 1964), p. 1013.
74. *Ibid.*
75. *Ibid.*
76. Harjinder Singh, (1976). *Authority and Influence in two Sikh Villages*, (New Delhi. Sterling Publishers, Pvt. Ltd.).
77. *Ibid.*
78. *Ibid.*
79. Saran, Parmatma, (1978). *Rural Leadership in the Context of India's Modernization*, (New Delhi, Vikas Publishing Pvt. Ltd.).
80. *Ibid.*
81. *Ibid.*
82. *Ibid.*

3

RESEARCH PROCEDURES

As stated earlier, the study is concerned with rural leadership and its social, educational and psychological correlates. The first chapter was devoted to a discussion of the significance of the problem of leadership with reference to villages. The social and historical account of the problem, the different dimensions used for the study of leadership, the increasing importance of the problem in the present context of planned social, economic and political changes in the country, and the need for empirical research by social scientists in this area, were discussed elaborately therein. The second chapter covered several researches undertaken in the past, employing different variables, to examine the relationship of these variables to rural leadership by way of a review. The present chapter is devoted to a discussion of the research procedures adopted in this study. The operational definitions of the concepts, the tools and techniques employed and the hypotheses formulated are presented here for a discussion of the rationale supporting the study. The problem of the present research may be restated here for clarity and for development of an appropriate procedure, thus: "A study of the social, educational and psychological background of the rural leaders and its relation to their democratic vs. authoritarian attitude".

Therefore, an attempt is made in this study to examine a few selected socio-psychological variables in relation to the democratic vs. authoritarian attitudes of the rural leaders. The general objectives of the study therefore are:

(1) to know the socio-economic background of the rural leaders with a view to examining whether the leadership is the privilege of certain sections of the village community,

(2) to know the influence of the levels of exposure to mass media and contacts with extension agency of the rural leaders on their democratic vs. authoritarian attitude.

(3) to find out the relationship between the levels of aspiration of rural leaders and their democratic vs. authoritarian attitude.

(4) to study the degree of social awareness among rural leaders and its relationship to their democratic attitude towards social problems.

Based on our discussion in the first chapter, we can presume several socio-psychological causes, which influence the emergence of leaders and their democratic vs. authoritarian attitude. The socio-economic status, the educational background, the political and group ideology, their receptiveness to new ideas, their rising levels of aspirations, their identity with the community and nation, the increasing degree of exposure to mass media and extension agency contacts, the level of social awareness in the context of social, economic and political changes in the country, their traditional vs. modern outlook in life, may be taken as some of the important factors influencing the rural leaders with reference to their democratic vs. authoritarian attitude. However, after careful scrutiny, the following four variables are selected to examine their relationship with democratic vs. authoritarian attitude of the rural leaders.

(1) Socio-economic status;

(2) Exposure to mass-media and extension agency contact;

(3) Levels of Aspiration; and

(4) Social awareness.

A discussion of these variables, depends on the meaning and definitions attached to the concepts that underlie these variables. It may, therefore, be considered necessary, to provide a brief discussion of the operational meanings of the concepts underlying these variables.

For a better understanding of the research problem it will be appropriate to know about the concepts of leader, leadership, types of leaders and their characteristics.

Meaning and Definition of Leaders and Leadership

Leader is a person who influences the activities of the group to which he belongs and who plays a central role in defining the group ideology and the group goals. The leader is denoted as an individual with a status that permits him to exercise influence over certain other individuals.[1]

In terms of group goal setting and goal achievement a leader has been defined as an individual who can exert influence upon the goal setting and goal achievement activities.[2]

Bernard Bass defined leadership as a kind of interaction between or among people. Any attempt on the part of a group member to change the behaviour of one or more members of a group is an attempt at leadership.[3]

Sociologists normally define leadership in terms of power, or the capacity of any individual in a social system to influence the behaviour of others. Davis considered power as the determination of the behaviour of others in accordance with one's ends.

According to Parsons, authority is a legitimate institution representing the institutionalised right of leaders to expect support from the members of a collectivity as well as the right to control and regulate their activities within the institutional framework.[4]

The literature dealing with the socio-psychological aspect of leadership emphasizes the ability of the leader to influence others to cooperate and identify a common purpose or goal. Tead observes, "leadership as the activity of influencing people to cooperate toward some goal which they come to find desirable."[5] Pigors views leadership as a process of mutual stimulation which, by the successful interplay of relevant individual differences, controls human energy in the pursuit of a common cause.[6]

Leadership as defined by Cartwright and Zander aims at maintaining the integration and continuity of the group structure. All members of the group contribute to the group's movement towards the satisfaction of its needs and wants, under the direction or guidance of the leader.[7] All members of the group interact and interdepend upon one another to achieve the set goals.[8]

Thus, leadership is essentially an interactional phenomenon between the leader and the follower. The relationship between the leaders and the followers is one of the several forms of interpersonal relationships which is formed to satisfy some of the defined needs of the leader and the followers, belonging to the same social system. Thus, the behaviour of one is generally influenced by the behaviour of the other, on the one hand, while the behaviour of both is determined by the nature and structure of the social system in which they interact.[9] Leadership is, therefore, a function of the three dimensions: (1) leader's personality traits, (2) leader's manner of communication with the followers and (3) perception of the leader by the followers as the satisfier of their needs and goals.[10]

By virtue of his ability to guide his group members, the leader occupies a special status in the group. He is considered to be the central figure by all, who find in him qualities which can help the members of the group to achieve the desired goals. Because of some functional abilities and special attitudes to perform certain group tasks, the leader is elevated to a higher position and comes to occupy a higher social status than other members of the group.[11] The high social rank of the leader and the respect that is accorded to him are also determined by the fact that he initiates interaction for the group by giving orders that are in fact obeyed.[12]

Theories of Leadership

Theories of leadership ranged all the way from Carlyl's great man theory through Pareto's organizational concepts of the rule of the elite, Spencer's deterministic model with emphasis on environmental order and finally, to theories that see leadership as diffused throughout the group. Each such theory however seems to have stressed some factor at the expense of others. For instance the early studies of leadership have focused on the leader himself, to determine the physical traits as compared to the followers.[13] But they could not make any substantial contribution to understand the dynamics of leadership. Gouldner[14] reviewed several studies in leadership and arrived at the conclusion that there was no evidence concerning the existence of universal leadership traits.

Dissatisfaction with the trait approach has then given rise to a view of leadership that stresses the characteristics of the group and the situation in which it exists. It is assumed that different situations require different kinds of leadership behaviour and the leadership is determined by the particular situation. Stogdill[15] having reviewed a number of leadership studies concludes, "the qualities, characteristics and skills required in a leader are determined to a large extent by the demands of the situation in which the individual is to function as a leader. Rossi and Hendry,[16] while reviewing the researches on leadership, have drawn attention to three theories of leadership: (1) great man or trait theory, (2) leadership as a function of the group and (3) leadership as a function of the situation in which the group is placed, and considered important to study all the three aspects of leadership for a better understanding. Gibbs states that the major variables in terms of which leadership must be understood are (1) the leader's personality, (2) the needs, attitudes and problems of the followers, (3) the group itself, in terms of both structure of inter-personal relations and syntality[17] characteristics and (4) the situation in terms of both the physical circumstances and the group task.

The literature reviewed in this study indicates that there is considerable agreement on the importance of the personality factors, cultural forces of situations and interactions in the understanding of the leadership process.

Characteristics of Leaders

There have been many efforts to document the distinct attributes of leadership. The differentiation between leaders and non-leaders is made depending on personal characteristics, the structure of interpersonal relationships and the general community settings.

Early studies of leadership emphasised the physical, intellectual and personality traits of the leaders as compared to the followers.

Some of the research studies indicated that the leaders' behaviour is distinguishable from non-leaders' behaviour, but no cluster of personality traits could be identified as distinguishing leaders from non-leaders.[18]

It has been admitted that an outstanding leader is to be credited with not only extension of the normal qualities possessed by most men but also with extraordinary powers such as the ability to read men's minds and to compel obedience.

Various studies on rural leadership in India have been concerned with the study of characteristics of leaders. Many such studies have focused on the personal (like age, physical appearance, abilities and qualities) and socio-economic characteristics (like caste, class, wealth, income, occupation, land ownership, social status and education).

Lewis[19] for instance found that the characteristics important for leadership were wealth, family reputation, personality traits, education, contacts and influence with outsiders.

Dube[20] in his study identified religion, caste, education, land ownership, wealth, position in village organisation and distinctive personality traits like the ability to talk persuasively, as important characteristics of leaders.

Similarly, besides education, caste and economic position, personal characteristics like simplicity, enthusiasm, sympathy were also considered as important characteristics for leadership.[21]

However, it is observed in several studies that the leader emerges as a result of possessing certain qualities such as, intelligence, ambition, personal adjustment, social participation, dependability, popularity, hospitality, self-confidence, will and generosity, impartiality, ability and high socio-economic status, and they excel non-leaders in these dimensions.[22] These qualities are found to characterise leaders of various types in various situations. No personality trait guarantees leadership in all situations. Studies of the relative frequency of various characteristics of both leaders and followers and studies of the generality or specificity of leadership form situation to situation and group to group, suggest that certain personality characteristics increase the likelihood of a person adopting the role of a leader or follower in a wide variety of situations.

The characteristics that are found to be important for rural leadership are: social status of the family, economic status based on land and wealth, religion, caste, education, ability to speak, hospitality and humility, intelligence and influence.[23]

In the light of the above theoretical discussion on the qualities and characteristics of leaders in general and the socio-cultural conditions under which the leaders have to provide direction to masses in the community in particular, it is felt that a leader in rural India need to be inductive, pragmatic and considerate. The leader should be one who has faith in material progress and can direct people towards modern procedures without creating obstructive antagonism. Considering the complex rural problems and deep-rooted cultural values of the people, the leaders in India should inspire people to accept changes, liberate them from traditional values of "Anasakti" and renunciation and prepare for a new social order built around the principles of social mobility.

Types of Leaders

Leaders are part of the essential mechanism of a group. They are the product of a situation. There cannot be a group without a leader. Sanderson and Polson have pointed out that every group would have within it the necessary leaders whether acknowledged or not. Every situation brings to the forefront some leader within the community. Potential and resourceful leadership is avilable in every community.

Leaders can be classified according to number of principles, such as area of life and thought in which they operate, type of control they exercise using the degree of contact.

Cecil A Gibb's[24] classification of leaders is based on a number of principles such as degree of contact of leaders with those who are led, mode of selection used in selecting leaders, leadership style or manner of exerting influences.

Max Weber classifies authority into charismatic, traditional and legal. Killian distinguishes three types of leadership in social movements—the charismatic leader, the administrative leader, and the intellectual leader. The charismatic leader simplifies and symbolises the values, the administrative leader promotes them, and the intellectual leader elaborates and justifies them by providing the ideology for the movement.

Basing on personal qualities Bogardus, classified leaders as mental, social, and executive leaders.[25] Mental leadership is qualified with intelligence and the capacity for abstract thought. Social Leadership is considered by Bogardus as the superior directing of associates. The characteristics implied here are social contact with followers, which may be expressed in self assertion. The leader is characterised with self-confidence, enthusiasm and extroversion. Executive leadership is a combination of social and mental forms of leadership. It is characterised with superior planning and conveying of plan into action. It calls for the invention of plans which do not refer to ideas but to actions. Bogardus[26] presents another classification in terms of (a) autocratic, (b) paternalisitc and (c) democratic leadership.

Autocratic leadership rules persons without consulting the group. The leader's attitude towards his followers is usually contemptuous.

Paternalistic form is distinguished from the above on the basis of the benevolence of the leader who genuinely works for the welfare of the people.

Democratic leadership is grown out of the needs of the group. The goal of the leader is the welfare of other people. The manner of coming to a decision is through consultation and discussion. The manner of implementing decisions is not by dictating but by setting example or by indirect sugestions.

Investigations in their studies of leadership in Indian villages have attempted to classify leadership into different types by using different criteria.

Dubey[27] and Guruswamy[28] have classified leaders into traditional, sectional, institutional, functional and professional.

1. *Traditional Leaders:* Here the leadership of the community is ascriptive.
2. *Sectional Leaders:* Sectional leaders are those whose influence extends only to particular sections of the community, *e.g.* Leaders of caste, factions, etc.
3. *Institutional Leaders:* Here the leadership is based on organised institutions such as panchayats and cooperatives.
4 *Functional Leaders:* Functional leaders are those whose influence comes from their individual specialities; people come to seek their advice and try to follow it.

5. *Professional Leaders:* These are the leaders who come usually from outside the village. Therefore, they may or may not be the members of the community, for example school teachers are professional leaders.

Treating prominence or importance as the basis, Dhillon classified leaders into three categories :

(1) Primary or major leaders,

(2) Secondary leaders and

(3) Tertiary or minor leaders.[29]

Primary leaders are those whose presence is considered essential in all important meetings of the village. Secondary leaders are those who occupy important positions in their respective factions. Tertiary leaders represent small kinship units.

Singh *et al*[30] classified leaders into traditional, political opinion-makers, decision-makers and caste leaders on the basis of sociometric choices. Bhouraskar[31] classified leadership structure into official and non-official which was further classified into formal and informal leadership. Salvi and Patil[32] classified leaders according to their origin into elected, appointed and sociometric choice. William McCormack[33] in his study classified leaders into three types—the traditional or hereditary leaders (villages ceremonial chief, members of the traditional village panchayat, the caste head man and the Patel) who claimed leadership on the hereditary principle, the wealthy leaders, who had no traditional or hereditary claim to leadership and the factional leaders who were non-hereditary. Orenstein[34] classified leaders as formal and informal leaders.

The studies which have been reviewed so for have reported various categories of leadership. A number of doubts has been raised in regard to the possibility of developing such typologies in Indian rural setting. It is held that in reality, village leaders in India cannot be classified into different categories as they are not so mutually exclusive. They usually possess overlapping characteristics, therefore, it is difficult to classify them.

Besides these shortcomings, in the light of above discussion, the investigator felt that the leaders could be classified broadly into two categories : (1) formal leaders. and (2) informal leaders.

OPERATIONAL DEFINITIONS

Formal Leaders and Informal Leaders

As stated earlier, investigators in their studies of leadership in Indian villages have attempted to classify leadership into different types by using different criteria. In the present investigation leaders have been classified into formal and informal leaders.

A formal leader, in this study, has been viewed as an authoritative figure who has the right and responsibility to act by virtue of the office he holds. Thus, all the members of the village Panchayat, including the Sarpanch, are considered as formal leaders.

Informal leader is viewed as one who commands respect and regard of the people by virtue of his individual specialities, his commitment to welfare of the people and his ability to provide direction to the followers.

Democratic vs. Authoritarian Attitude

Democratic vs. authoritarian behaviour in the present investigation, is restricted to certain qualities of behaviour of leaders in situations that are generally associated with rural life.

The most common form of classification of leaders has been in terms of leadership style or manner of exerting influence, and the terms generally used to designate the opposing poles of this continuum are "autocratic" (authoritaranism) and "democatic" leadership. Most of the studies of leaders' behaviour have been concerned with the leaders' attitude towards the principle of "authoritarinism vs. democratic behaviour". In the former the leader tends to centralise and sometimes even monopolise the decision-making process, whereas in the latter the decisions are arrived at by the group members, and the role of the leader being that of evolving maximum group participation. Consensus for task tends to be represented by authoritarian leader's behaviour while a consensus for relationships is represented by democratic leader's behaviour. This feeling was popular among past writers because it was generally the two ways (i) he can tell his followers what to do and how to do it or (ii) he can share his leadership responsibilities with his followers by involving them in the planning and execution of the task. The former is the traditional authoritarian style which emphasizes task consensus. The latter, the more non-directive democratic style, stresses the consensus for human relationships.

The authoritarian leadership has been described by Lippit[35] *et. al.*, as follows:

(1) All determination of policy is made by the leaders;

(2) Techniques and steps for attaining the goal are dictated by the leaders;

(3) The leader usually dictates work tasks and work companions of each member;

(4) The leader is personal in his praise and criticism without giving objective reasons;

(5) The leader remains relatively aloof from group participation.

McGregor[36] has spelled out the assumptions on which this approach is based, namely, (1) the average human being has an inherent dislike for work and will avoid it if he can, (2) because of this human characteristic of dislike for work people must be coerced, controlled, directed and threatened with punishment to make them to put forth adequate effort towards the achievement of organizational objectives, and directed, wishes to avoid responsibility, has relatively little ambition, wants security above all.

By contrast, the democratic leadership style emphasizes an entirely different approach. Democratic leadership is, in most respects the direct antithesis of the authoritarian pattern described above. It is associated mainly with relationship in which there are shared satisfactions and a mutual respect of leader and led for one another.[37]

Lippit[38] *et. al.*, have defined the democratic leadership as follows:

(1) Policies are formulated by group decisons;

(2) The explanation of the over all process is given at the first meeting;

(3) If technical advice is needed, the leaders give several alternatives from which a choice can be made;

(4) Members are free to choose work companions and division of tasks;

(5) Leaders are objective in their praise and criticism and try to be regular group members themselves in spirit and in practice, although they are often prevented from doing the actual work of a member.

The democratic leader has the complex problems of giving each individual satisfaction as an individual, protecting the group as a whole, and satisfying his own aspirations and benevolent intentions. He does not necessarily differ from the authoritarian leader in the amount or extent of his power, but he has a different role or pattern of roles in the group structure.[39]

"Democratic leader seeks to evoke the maximum involvement and the participation of every member in the group activities and in the determination of objectives. He seeks to spread responsibility rather than to concentrate it. He seeks to encourage and reinforce interpersonal contacts and relationism, throughout the group structure so as to strengthen it. He seeks to reduce intra-group tension and conflict. He seeks to avoid hierachical group structure in which special privilege and status differentials predominate".[40]

McGregor[41] has suggested the following aspects as the bases of the democratic leadership; (1) the expenditure of physical and mental effort in work is as natural as play or rest; (2) external control and threat of punishment are not the only means for bringing about effort towards organizational objectives. A man will exercise self-direction and self-control, in the service of objectives to which he is committed; (3) commitment to objectives is a function of the rewards associated with their achievement; (4) the average human being learns under proper conditions, not only to accept, but to seek responsibility; (5) the capacity to exercise a relatively high degree of imagination, ingenuity and creativity in the solution of organization problems is widely distributed in the population; (6) under the conditions of modern life, the intellectual potentialities of the average human being are only partially utilized.

One of the principal advantages of the democratic technique is its evocation of maximum participation from all group members. It is an educational axiom that persons understand more fully those things they have themselves experienced, and they grasp more completely those ideas in the formulation of which they have participated.[42]

Group discussions which have been arrived at by group members interactively, and as a synthesis of their own efforts, elicit more solid support and issue into action more frequently than to those which are handed down authoritatively.[43]

Because it shares decision making and other responsibilities, democratic leadership enables a group to make maximum use of the relevant individual differences existing within it. It releases creativity in group members because it can tolerate temporary or specific transfer of power and influence in a way that authoritarianism cannot.[44]

Cohesiveness or viscidity of a group is found to be generally higher under conditions of democratic leadership.[45]

Thus, the two types of leadership have been defined and differentiated. It is extremely difficult to evaluate the relative contribution that each type or style of leadership makes to the actual attainment of group goals. It appears that democratic leadership tends to maintain a higher level of motivation in all the group members than authoritarian leadership. One fact that seems to be relatively well established is that, at the beginning, everybody seems to assume that it is the task of the leader to assume full responsibility for the work, development and success of the group. It takes time and experience to realise that the attainment of the goal is everybody's business. There is evidence to indicate that authoritarian leadership is welcomed when the group is under emotional strain and feels insecure. Some are of the view that adoption of authoritarian leadership is more effective, particularly in a tradition bound country like India, to change faster and to strike harder at the social and economic evils.

But we assume the leaders to be democratic in their behaviour as we are committed to a philosophy of socio-economic and political democracy. Since the objectives of community development and Panchayati Raj are maximising participation of every member in the activities and determination of objectives, the democratic leader seeks to distribute responsibility rather than to concentrate it. He seeks to encourage and reinforce interpersonal contacts and relationships throughout the group structure so as to strengthen it. Group decisions, which have been arrived at by group members interactively, and as a synthesis of their own efforts, elicit more solid support. As discussed above, in the present day context the leaders should be democratic in their attitude and they should participate and accelerate the process of democratization in the community. On the contrary, if the rural leaders are, traditional, conservative and authoritarian it may be difficult to implement most of the development programmes in the rural community. In the light of this discussion, an attempt is made in this study to investigate the the rural leader's democratic vs. authoritarian attitude.

Studies on leadership indicate a wide variety of styles of leader's behaviour between these two extremes. Robert Tannenbaum[46] depicted a broad range of styles on a continuum moving from authoritarian leader behaviour at one end to democratic leader behaviour at the other. A leader may not have democratic outlook and behaviour in all situations. In some situations he may be democratic and in some other autocratic.

In the present investigation the leader behaviour is studied and measured on a continuum, with authoritarianism and democracry at the extreme poles. Authoritarianism and democracy are restricted to certain modes of behaviour of rural leaders in situations that are generally faced by the leaders. Leaders who wield unlimited power to influence their followers without taking group's concern, who tries to maintain their status quo, who resist the changes and who are interested in individual benefit are considered authoritarian leaders. Leaders who exert limited leadership, show inclination towards social, economic and political equality, have positive and favourable outlook towards new institutions, socio-economic and political changes and who are interested in working for group benefit are treated as democratic leaders.

Socio-Economic Status

Socio-economic status as an important variable of leadership has been established by several researchers in the past. Leadership is held by persons belonging to the higher echelons of the village community which has been well documented in a number of community studies. Most of the studies[47] on institutional leadership, have related socio-economic background as the determinant of leadership pattern. These studies revealed that village leadership is the privilege of certain sections of the village community. It is observed that village leaders generally had a higher income, landholding, cattle, wealth and belonged to higher caste. The findings of such studies in a way suggest that the elected leaders of the village Panchayat are by and large, those who had some ascribed status in the village because of their personal resources.[48] It may also be said that the traditional leaders have become elected leaders with the creation of village Panchayats.[49] It is a matter of interest to explore the extent to which the introduction of village Panchayats, and social, economic and political changes provided opportunities for the emergence of new leadership based on achieved status in the community rather than ascribed status particularly in Andhra Pradesh. So far there is no clear cut evidence to know whether the socio-economic background of the leaders influences their attitude towards democratic vs. authoritarian behaviour. In this context it is necessary to examine which level of socio-economic background is associated with the development of democratic attitude among the rural leaders. It is, therefore, considered as an important area for exploration in the present study which attempts to identify the level of socio-economic status, from which the leaders emerge, and its relationship to their democratic attitude.

For the purpose of measuring socio-economic background of the leaders, the problem was to construct an appropriate index of socio-economic status. Several studies in the past by Vijay Pratap Singh,[50] Pareek,[51] have suggested caste, landed property, political power, education and occupation as important factors for social stratification and for identifying socio-economic status of rural population. Kuppu Swamy[52] has included education, income and occupation as necessary factors for identifying the socio-economic status of urban population.

Community studies done in India, especially the recent diffusion studies have used age, family size, caste, rank, income, education, as the major elements in the index of socio-economic status.

It has been found in the studies of the social scientists like Mehta,[53] Sirsikar,[54] Bada,[55] Ram Reddy and Seshadri,[56] that caste, education, occupation, income and land holding were important determinants of leadership pattern in rural villages of India. Therefore, in developing a suitable index for socio-economic status in the present study, the following components have been included.

1. Caste,
2. Educational level,
3. Occupation,
4. Income level,
5. Land holdings,
6. Type of house and
7. Social participation.

It is universally agreed that educational level, occupation, income level, land holding, type of house, social participation are important factors in determining the socio-economic status of a person. In addition to this, the position of the individual in the caste hierarchy is also included in this study for the following reasons.

The position of the respondents in the traditional caste hierarchy of our society, measured in terms of forward castes, backward castes, and scheduled castes, is included in this study. The relationship between caste superiority and authority has been an important theme in all sociological treatises on Indian Society. Traidtionally superior castes had the upper hand in society; leadership was the monopoly of the upper caste. It has been observed that the socially influentials usually stemmed from higher castes who were ritually superior and economically better off than the vast majority of middle and lower classes. Important role, in traditional leadership, was generally concentrated in the hands of the elite castes. Because of the historical and traditional importance given to the caste hierarchy, it is assumed in the present study that the caste plays an important factor in determining the leadership position.

Thus, in the present study, for the reasons explained above, the seven sub-variables—caste, level of education, occupation, income level, land holdings, types of house, social participation of the respondents are included in the index of socio-economic status.

Exposure to Mass Media and Extension Agency Contacts

Social change may be the result of internal forces and processes, whether planned or spontaneous, or it may be produced by external factors like environment and contact with foreign cultures. The former types may be called immanent change and the latter external change. External or contact change may be directed or non-directed. Spontaneous change occurs where members of a social system adopt new ideas that have been unintentionally or spontaneously communicated to them by outsiders. Directed, contact change is a developmental change with implications for deliberate, planned, and purposive social action. Extension agencies in developing societies represent the dominant change agent system with well defined goals and definite strategy of social action.

The extension service in India is the principal source of modernizing messages in rural communities. Agents of change concentrate their interpersonal communication on those who are most responsive and influential. These agents locate and train and work with the local leaders who can influence and carry conviction to their fellow villagers. Rogers[57] has demonstrated that most of the change agents have greater contact with community influentials who are characterised by greater innovativeness, higher social status and more education than their counterparts. The importance of community leaders can be analysed in three ways. The messages communicated by the community leaders are perceived as trustworthy by the villagers. As Ithial Pool[58] points out, in traditional societies a message will not be accepted unless it comes from the right oracle. Secondly, the community leaders are the key persons who legitimize any changes, proposed by extension agents. Thirdly, programme planning and execution at the local level will depend on the initiative, and enthusiasm of community leaders. Community leaders mobilize the community into action and carry the project to its completion. The involvement of the local influentials in these community projects enhance their prestige and reputation. Contact with extension agents is a mark of superiority, and those who have greater contact with change agents are more likely to be chosen to represent the community.

Mass media is deemed to be a catalytic agent in the modernization process. Rogers[59] has termed mass media exposure as the "magic multiplier", for it is a broadener of horizons, an informer and a persuader for change. Newspapers, magazines, movies, radio and television open the window on the world. Several studies have demonstrated that mass media exposure is positively related to empathy, innovativeness, political knowledge, achievement motivation, education and occupational aspirations and other indices of modernization. It is generally conceded that mass media plays a significant role in the process of modernization. Exposure to mass media–radio, movies, newspaper–is also an index of linkage with an external system,

As it is noted that the leaders at the grassroots are the key persons for implementation and success of programmes of planned change, it is necessary that these leaders must be equipped with greater knowledge and progressive ideas. In a rapidly changing society like ours, leaders who blaze new paths of thought and action and who can enthuse others are required at various situations. These leaders should have the perception of social changes occurring in the society. They should be aware of the attitudes, aspirations and patterns of behaviour of the society in which they operate. In this connection the leader should have higher social contacts and greater level of exposure to mass media.

Exposure to mass media facilitates progressive orientation and broader social contacts. Extension agency contact will enable them to have a favourable outlook towards the changes that are brought in our society. Both together broaden the horizon of knowledge of the individual. Exposure to mass media is regarded as an index of expertise because of its high potential for enrichment of knowledge and competence of the individual. These people keep abreast with current affairs.

In the light of the above discussion, an attempt is made in this investigation to study the degree of exposure to mass media and extension agency contacts of the rural leaders. An attempt is also made to investigate the influence of the exposure of the leaders to mass media and extension agency contacts on their democratic vs. authoritarian attitude.

For operational purpose, in the present investigation, listening radio, reading a newspaper, reading a magazine, attendance at movies are taken as exposure to mass media, and contacts with village level workers, extension officers, community development officials *etc*, are taken as extension agency contacts.

Aspiration Levels

After the independence of India, a number of steps were directed by the government towards improving the well-being of the people and inducing thereby social change in the society. The main objective of the planned programmes was to make the people raise their standard of living and also raise the expectations of the masses, under the assumption that increased expectations would lead to putting in increased efforts for better life. In this connection, leaders who serve as a link between the policy-makers and the rural masses, should have higher levels of aspirations to raise the expectations of the masses.

Study of aspiration level will give an understanding of the trend of social mobility in a given society.[60] These aspirations or expectations could be towards education, income, occupation or any such thing that may be necessary for a bright future. Studies undertaken to study the aspirations of leaders are very few. Hardly any studies have been undertaken so far to find the influence of the rising levels of aspiration among rural leaders on their democratic attitude.

Therefore, an attempt is made in this investigation to examine the levels of aspirations of the rural leaders in relation to their democratic vs. authoritarian attitude.

Aspirations are goal statements concerning future level of achievement. Levels of aspirations, as commonly entertained, include a variety of tendencies. By some it is regarded as an individual's conception of his future propspects, and a few others viewed aspiration as a form of self-motivation.[61] In this sense aspiration is regarded as an individual's expectations of his future performance and accomplishments or a desire to accomplish. An aspiration thus usually refers to a person's or a group of persons' orientation towards a goal.[62]

One commonly accepted definition of the level of aspiration is "the degree to which the individual sets his goals realistically in relation to his physical and mental attributes, and in accordance with his environment."[63] Cronbach, defined level of aspiration as "the level of performance or the goal that a person (or a group) desires or hopes to reach in a specified activity".[64] Goals can vary in kind and are usually described with reference to a particular social status or status attribute (occupation, income, education, residence and so on). Higher and lower levels of aspiration are used to indicate relative level of goal specifications; strong and weak aspirations are used to describe the relative intensity of the orientation element. For the present investigation in the context of the above discussion, the following operational definition of aspiration is accepted : *Aspiration is the goal or level of attainment that an individual likes to reach for his success in life.*

Social Awareness

Since independence many changes have taken place in our society. The process of change has been accelerated with the introduction of planned massive programmes to realize better standard of socio-economic life and for the uplift of the socially handicapped through the existing political system. Today most of the developmental programmes are looking for new leadership in rural areas which could transmit the message, mobilize people's support and intensify their participation.

The role of a leader in this context is crucial. A leader today must be a person endowed with a wide social perspective, sensitivity to human unity and imbued with strong sense of social responsibility. He must be free from the corruption of prejudices and narrow loyalties. He should have a sincere enthusiasm for democratic life.[65] Further, he must possess a certain degree of qualities such as intelligence, personal adjustment, sociability, dominance and interpersonal sensitivity together with the ability to perceive social change and the determination of making the required changes to meet the new situation.[66] The leader should possess broad and general knowledge of people and their cultures, at least the cultural, social, political and economic development of his own country, awareness of some contemporary issues, a special knowledge of democratic techniques. A leader should have the necessary awareness of the social, economic and political changes, perceptible and imperceptible, taking place at all levels of community in order to guide and provide direction to his followers on the right lines. The leader, being a socially acceptable individual will be sensitive to what is going on in the society and accepts the necessary changes. Unless there is an amount of awareness on the part of the leaders regarding these changes as desirable and possible, it may be difficult to translate many of these national and community programmes into action.

Leaders' attitude to conformity and change need to be studied in depth, emphasis must be given to their views about changes and their interests in change. In relation to specific items of change, it would be useful to discover how the proposed changes hurt or further their vested interests. Therefore, the present study aims at studying the social awareness of rural leaders. The concept of awareness has been viewed by many in the past as knowledge about, things, happenings, institutions *etc.*

Awareness was measured in past researches, at cognitive level *i.e.* they investigated whether people were aware of the changes that were occurring in the society. They also investigated whether the people were aware of the policies that were implemented.[67] In some studies the knowledge regarding social and economic changes is studied by analyzing their attitudes towards these changes as attitudinal surveys.

In the present study awareness is not limited to cognitive level information about the existence of new institution and prevalence of changes, but it is conceived as "problem consciousness" implying a desire on the part of the leaders to overthrow traditional injustices and create a new social order.

Social awareness is viewed as that knowledge which helps a man in realization of the fact that modern institutions, ways of life, new policies designed to bring radical changes are created to the advantage of the common man, and living according to these institutional ways and philosophy is not only desirable but also possible. Therefore social awareness is defined in this study as knowledge about the new institutions, social, economic and political changes and the inclination towards achieving these change (change of outlook). Social awareness is charactarised by the following dimensions.

(a) Their knowledge about the existence of the new institutions and changes.

(b) Their attitude about the desirability of these changes and new institutions.

(c) Their feeling regarding the possibility of attaining these changes—this three level information put together will be known as the social awareness of the individual.

Statement of Hypotheses

The present study is designed to investigate empirically the background of rural leaders, in terms of their *socio-economic status, exposure to mass media and extension agency contact, levels of aspiration and social awareness* and the relationship of each one of these four independent variables to their *democratic vs. authoritarian attitude*. In order to examine the relationship of each one of these variable to the principal variable *i.e.* democratic vs. authoritarian attitude four hypotheses have been formulated. The statements of these hypotheses, and the rationale on which they are based are presented in the following pages.

Hypothesis-I

With a view to examining the relationship between socio-economic status and the democratic vs. authoritarian attitude of the rural leaders the following hypothesis was formulated.

The higher the level of socio-economic status of the respondents the greater is the degree of their democratic attitude

The rationable for the formulation of the above hypothesis lies in the fact that socio-economic status of the individuals plays a predominant role in determining leadership. Traditionally, it has been observed that the authority structure in Indian villages had largely been ascriptive. Leadership was vested in persons belonging to certain privileged strata of society. Leadership position was occupied by higher caste who were ritually superior and economically better off.[68]

However, it is observed that western mode of education, industrialization, urbanization improved communication, and social legislations had their impact on the traditional structure of Indian community. The pace of change has been increased with the introduction of community development, Panchayati Raj and Cooperatives.[69]

These forces of change did not leave the leadership structure untouched. In this context, a considerable transformation is noticed in the pattern of leadership.[70] The pattern of rural leadership as it exists today reflects a transition from the hereditary and ascriptive to democratic and achievement oriented type. The new forces are specifically effective in changing the composition of rural leadership with regard to the factors of age,[71] income,[72] education[73] and caste.[74] Some studies have pointed out the emergence of young educated leaders in rural areas.[75]

Though a considerable transformation is evinced in the leadership pattern, it is also observed in some villages that caste, economic position and land holding, continue to be the bases of the leadership with varying degrees of influence in different areas.[76]

In this context it is also to be noted that the leader with high socio-economic status is generally perceived in a rural area as a spokesman of the community, and as a liaison between the local community and policy makers.[77]

Such leaders might keep themselves well informed of current affairs. They are also better recipients of the flow of information from outside. As the members of the upper strata of the society, their opportunities of exposure to the recent changes might influence their outlook towards democratic vs. authoritarian style of functioning.

The studies in the past have indicated that in the case of activists[78] who generally emerge as leaders with an attitude towards righteousness and indignant behaviour, there was a positive relationship between their levels of activism and socio-economic status. As, righteousness and indignant behaviour are important components of democratic attitude it may be understood in the same token that there could be a positive relationship between socio-economic status and democratic vs. authoritarian behaviour of the leaders. Thus the hypothesis that "there is a positive relationship between the socio-economic status and the democratic attitude of the rural leaders" is formulated.

Hypothesis-II

In order to examine the relationship between the media exposure and extension agency contacts of the rural leaders and their democratic vs. authoritarian attitude, the following hypothesis is formulated:

Greater the degree of extension agency contact and media exposure, higher is their democratic attitude

In a country that is under the influence of planned and directed change, contacts with extension agency and media exposure must turn out to be crucial variables in predicting community leadership. In rural India community development and extension agency represent the major forces of social change. The philosophy of change agents is to identify, develop and depend on community leadership. So those having higher level of contacts with extension agents stand a better chance for emerging as leaders. So also with the media exposure. Mass media is deemed to be a catalytic agent in the modernization process. There is a general agreement among communication experts and developmental planners on mass media's role in achieving a climate for modernisation. It serve as a link with external system. Exposure to mass media, especially the radio and the press, enriches the knowledge and competence of an individual. With its high potentiality it may be regarded as an index of expertise. So in the context of modernizing Indian villages, community members' exposure to mass media can brighten their chance of being elected to the places of responsibility. Thus, extension agency contact and exposure to mass media play a crucial role in determining leadership.

In the past many investigators considered these two variables to determine leadership position. Abraham[79] in his study found a positive and significant correlation between extension agency contact, newspaper exposure, and community leadership.

While analysing the characteristics of emergent leaders, Pradipto Roy,[80] noted that the leaders had higher level of contact with extension agencies. Sen and Roy[81] observed that the leaders had greater contact with extension agency and exposure to newspaper reading. Fliegel[82] and others observed that the extension agency contact was one of the most important determinants of village leadership.

Studies have been conducted by Dasgupta,[83] Sen,[84] Nirmalakant Saha[85] to mention a few, comparing the characteristics of the rural leaders with those of their followers. They have pointed out that the leaders had greater contact with extension agency, and greater exposure to mass media than the non-leaders.

In the present study an attempt is also made to find the degree of contact with extension agency and exposure to mass media among the rural leaders.

The contacts with extension agency and exposure to mass media broaden the horizon of knowledge of rural leaders and keep them abreast of changing value in the context of our social transformation from authoritarian social order to modern democratic social order.

In the light of this discussion, the hunch of the present investigator is that greater contacts with extension agency and media exposure influence the leaders to have a democratic outlook.

So in this study it is assumed that a greater contact with extension agency and media exposure would influence the leaders to have democratic attitude.

Hypothesis-III

In order to examine the relationship between the levels of aspiration and the degree of democratic attitude of the rural leaders the following hypothesis was formulated:

Greater the levels of aspiration, higher is the degree of democratic attitude.

Though there was no empirical evidence showing the relationship between the leaders' levels of aspiration and their democratic behaviour, an attempt is made in this study to find out the relationship between these two variables. The rationale for this assumption lies in the fact that the leaders' aspirations will depend on their belief in an open competition in an "open society" based on principle of equality and merit.

Secondly, India, like any other industrialising and modernising societies, believes in emphasising and encouraging high aspiration for its success. As stated earlier the main objectives of the planned programmes of change is: to make the people develop their standard of living and also to raise the expectation of the masses. In this context leaders who serve as a link between the policy- makers and the rural masses should have higher levels of aspiration towards future to raise the expectation of the masses. Individual mobility orientation, therefore, should have been deeply rooted among leaders as a concomitant of their belief in democratic way of living and working.

Attempts were made in the past to study the aspirations of rural leaders, in terms of their future leadership, higher leadership position,[86] economic position, their children's future education. It was discussed that the leaders had progressive and positive aspirations

Therefore, it is hypothesised that the leaders having positive and progressive aspirations believe in democratic social order to achieve their expected goals.

Hypothesis-IV

In order to examine the relationship between the levels of social awareness of rural leaders and their democratic attitude the following hypothesis is formed:

Higher the level of social awareness of the leaders, greater would be their democratic attitude.

The rationale behind the formulation of this hypothesis is that the knowledge of the new political and economic ideologies and social changes will influence the leaders to have a modern outlook which ultimately leads to have democratic attitude.

The role of the leader as a key person in developmental process assumed greater significance, in the context of our massive programmes to attain social change and to realise better standards of socio-economic life. Small communities are confronted with modern ways of life, new political and economic ideologies, scientific and technological innovations and sophisticated cultural patterns and social values. In this context the rural leader has to play a crucial role in seeking co-operation and maximising the participation of the masses. Therefore, leaders endowed with necessary awareness of social problems can alone guide and direct the masses towards democratic ways of living. Thus the study formulated the following hypothesis:

> *Higher the level of social awareness of the leaders, greater would be their democratic attitude.*

In the foregoing pages the hypotheses formulated for the present study with rationale for each hypothesis, have been discussed. Now a brief account of the sampling procedure adopted in the present study has been attempted in the following chapter.

Notes and References

1. Hollander, E.P. (1963). *Leaders, Groups and Influence,* (New York. Oxford University Press,), p.46.
2. Ralph. H. Stogdill, "Leadership Membership and Organization". In *The Study of Leadership,* (ed.) Browne, C.G. and Thomas S. Cohn, 1st ed. (Illinois. Printers and Publishers, Inc. 1959), p.33.
3. Bass Bernard M. (1960). *Leadership, Psychology and Organizational Behaviour,* (New York. Harper and Row,).
4. Parsons Talcott (1951). *The Social System,* (New York. Free Press).
5. Ordway Tead, (1963). *The Art of Leadership,* (New York. McGraw Hill Book Co.,), p. 20.
6. Paul Pigors, (1935). *Leadership of Domination,* (Boston, Houghton Mittlin Co.,), p. 16.
7. Darwin Cartwright and Alvin Zander (eds.). *Group Dynamics: Research and Theory,* Evanston, (Illinois. Row Peterson Co., 1956), p.538.

8. Murray G. Ross and Charles E. Hendry, (1957). *New Understanding of Leadership, A Survey and Application of Research,* (New York: Association Press,), p.83.
9. David Krech and Richard S. Crutchfield, (1948). *Theory and Problem of Social Psychology,* (N.Y., McGraw-Hill Book Co.,), p.401.
10. Darwin Cartwright and Alvin Jander (eds.). *op.cit.*
11. Murray G. Rose and Charles E. Hendry. *New Understanding of Leadership, A Survey and Application of Research, op.cit.*
12. George C. Homans, (1950). *The Job of the Leader, The Human Group,* (New York. HarCourt, Brace and World, Inc.,).
13. For related views see Cecil A. Gibb, "The Principles and Traits of Leadership", *Journal of Abnormal and Social Psychology,* Vol.XIII, (July, 1947), pp.267-84.
14. Alvin Gouldner (ed). *Studies in Leadership,* (New York. Harper and Brothers, 1950), p.31.
15. Stogdill R.M., "Personal Factors Associated with leadership—A Survey of literature". In *The Study of Leadership,* (ed.) Brown, C.G. and Thomas S.Cohn, *op.cit.*, pp. 50-61.
16. Murray G. Ross and Charles E. Hendry. *New Understanding of Leadership: A Survey and Application of Research, op.cit.*,
17. (i) Cecil A. Gibb, "Leadership". In *International Encyclopedia of the Social Sciences,* (ed.), David L. Sills (New York; the Macmillan Co. and the Free Press, 1968), Vol.9, pp.90-101.
    (ii) Also see. Cecil A. Gibb, "Leadership". In *Hand Book of Social Psychology,* ed. Gardner Lindzey, Vol.II (London: Addison—Wesley Publishing Company, Inc., 1959), pp.913-16.
18. Gerald R. Firth, (1970). "Theories of Leadership, Where Do We stand", *Educational Leadership,* 43, (N. 5, February), p.237.
19. Oscar Lewis, (1958). *Village Life in Northern India,* (Urbana. University of Illinois Press). p.127.
20. Dube, S.C., (1967). *Indian Village,* (New York. Harper and Row,),p.161.
21. Salvi, P.V. and Patil, R.Y., (1968). "Rural Local Leadership", *Rural India,* 31, No. 9, (November), pp. 343-45.
22. (i) Srivastava S.K., "Directed Social Change and Rural Leadership in India". In Leela Dube (ed) *Emerging Patterns of Rural Leadership in Southern Asia,* (Hyderabad. National Institute of Community Development, 1965), pp.151-71.
    (ii) Udai Pareek *et.al.* "Behavioural Characteristics of Effective Village Leaderships as Reported by Non-Leader Farmers", *Studies in Rural Leadership,* ed. Udai Pareek (Delhi: Behavioural Sciences Centre, 1966), pp.61-74.
    (iii) Pradipto Roy, "Participation in New Social Structure and Leadership". In ed, Leela Dube, *op.cit.* pp.135-49.

23. Indra P. Singh, "Leadership in a Sikh Village", *Leadership and Political Institutions in India,* ed. Park and Tinker, (Princeton. Princeton University Press, 1959), pp.321-31.

24. Cecil A. Gibb, "Leadership". In *International Encyclopedia of Social Sciences,* ed., David L. Sills (New York, the Macmillan Co. & the Free Press, 1968), Vol.9, pp.90-101.

25. Emory S. Bogardus, (1934). *Leaders and Leadership,* (New York. Appleton-Century Crofts, Inc.), p.15-33.

26. Emory S. Bogardus, (1934) Leaders and Leadership, *(New York: Appleton—Century Crofts, Inc.),* p.5-33.

27. Dubey S.C.,. "Leaders and Local Groups", *Summary of Talk* (University of Saugar).

28. Guruswamy M.P., "Local Leadership in Rural Development", *Khadi Gramodyog,* (August, 1960), p. 688.

29. Dhillon H.S., *Leadership and Groups in South Indian Village,* (Delhi. Planning Commission, P.E.O. 1953), pp.115-16.

30. Singh, *et. al,* "Different Types of Local Leadership in Two North Indian Villages". In *Studies in Rural Leadership,* ed. Udai Pareek, (Delhi. Behavioural Sciences Centre, 1966), pp.1-22.

31. Bhouraskar, K.M., "Leadership in "Tribal Village", *Man in India,* 44, No. 4. (October-December, 1964), pp. 329-40.

32. Salvi, P.V. and Patil R.Y. "Rural Local Leadership", *Rural India,* 31, No. 9, (November,1968), pp. 343-45.

33. William McCormack, "Factionalism in a Mysore Village". In *Leadership and Political Institution in India,* ed. Park and Tinker, *op.cit.,* pp.438-44.

34. Orenstein A, "Leadership and Caste in Bombay Village". *In Leadership and Political Institutions in India* (ed.) Park and Tinker, *op.cit.,* pp.415-26.

35. Ronald Lippitt and Ralph White, `Leader behaviour and member reaction in three social climates". In *Group Dynamics* (ed) Darwin Cartwright and Alvin Zander (New York. Harper and Row Publishers), pp. 318-35.

36. Quoted from J. Filella, S.J., "The Psychology of Leadership". In *The Nature of Leadership,* ed. J.W. Airan, (Bombay: Lalvani Publishing House), pp. 60-61.

37. Cecil A. Gibb, "Leadership". In *Hand Book of Social Psychology (ed)* Gardner Lindzey (London. Addison Wesley Publishing Co., 1954), p. 908.

38. Ronald Lippit and Ralph White "Leadership Behaviour and Member Reaction in Three Social Climates'. In *Group Dynamics (ed)* Darwin Cartwright and Alvin Zander, *op.cit.,*

39. Cecil A. Gibb, *"Leadership".* In *Hand Book of Social Psychology, op.cit.* p. 909.

40. Krech. D and Crutchfield, R.S., (1948). *Theory and Problems of Social Psychology,* (New York: McGraw Hill), p.426.

41. McGregor (quoted in) J.Filella, S.J."The Psychology of Leadership". In *The Nature of Leadership,* (ed) J.W. Airan, *op.cit.*

42. Cecil A. Gibb, "Leadership". In *Hand Book of Social* Psychology, ed. Gardner, Lindzey, *op.cit.*, p.910.
43. *Ibid.*
44. *Ibid.* pp. 910-11.
45. *Ibid.*.
46. Tannenbaum Robert, *et.al* "*Leadership and Organization—A Behavioural Science Approach*", (New York. McGraw Hill Book Company,Inc.1961).
47. (i) Harjinder Singh, *Village Leadership*, (Delhi. Sterling Publishers, 1967).
    (ii) Sirsikar V.M., *Rural Elite in Developing Society, op.cit.*,
    (iii) Neeladri Raju, "The Emerging Elite in Rural India—A Comparative Study of Elites in Andhra Pradesh, Maharashtra and West Bengal", *Behavioural Sciences and Community Development*, Vol. 5, No.1, (March-1972).
    (iv) Ram Reddy G. and Seshadri, K., "The Voter and Panchayat Raj—"A Study of the Electoral Behaviour During Panchayat Elections in Warangal and Andhra Pradesh, *op.cit*.
    (v) Singh, M. P. and Misra, R.P., "Characteristics of Village Leadership". In *Interdiscipline*, Vol. 10 No.3 (Summer-1973).
48. Muthayya, B.C., and Neeladri Raju K., "Personal and Social Background of Elected Village Leaders", *Community Development and Panchayat Raj Digest*, Vol. 4, No. 3, (January-1973).
49. *Ibid.*
50. Singh, Vijay Pratap—*The Evolution of Rural Stratification Systems in India* (1930-65)". Ph.D. thesis submitted to the University of Wisconsin 1970, quoted in Dr. M. Malla Reddy, *A Few Socio-Psychological Correlates of Student Activism*, Thesis submitted to Osmania University, p.87.
51. Pareek U. and Trivedi, G., "Reliability and Validity of a Rural Socio-Economic Status Scale", *Indian Journal of Applied Psychology*, 1-(1), (1964), pp.34-40.
52. Kuppu Swamy B, "A Scale to Measure Socio-Economic Status", *Indian Journal of Psychology*, Vol.34, (1959), pp.1-10.
53. Mehata S. R., *Emerging Pattern of Rural Leadership*, (Bombay: Wiley Eastern, 1972).
54. Sirsikar V.M.. "*Rural Elite in Developing Society*", *op.cit.*
55. Bada C.R.. "*Village Panchayat Key Leadership Pattern*. In *Interdiscipline, op.cit.*
56. Ram Reddy and Seshadri, *Voter and Panchayat Raj, op.cit.*
57. Rogers, Evert. M., *Diffusion of Innovation—Modernization among peasants. The Impact of Communication*, (New York: Reinehart and Winston Inc., 1969).
58. Pool Ithial de Sola, "The Mass Media and Their Inter-Personal Social Functions in the Process of Modernization". In Dexter and White (ed), *People, Society and Mass Communications*, (Glenco Free Press, 1954), pp.429-43.
59. Rogers, Evert M., *op.cit.*

60. (i) Sewell, W.H. and Shah V.P. "Social Class, Parental Encouragement and Educational Aspirations", *American Journal of Sociology*, (1968), 77(5), pp.559-72.

    (ii) Shah V.P. *et al.*, Social Class and Educational Aspirations in an Indian "Metropolis", *Sociological Bulletin*, Vol.XX, No.2, (September-1971), pp. 113--33.

61. Preston, M.G. and Bayton J.A., "Differential effect of a social variable upon three levels of aspiration", *Journal of Experimental Psychology*, 1941, pp. 29, 351, 361.

62. Haller, A.O., "On the concept of aspirations", *Rural Sociology*, 33 (4) (1968), pp. 484--87.

63. Carter V. Good, "Foundations in Education," (Dictionary of Education) Quoted. In Dr. M. Malla Reddy, *A Few Socio-Psychological Correlates of Student Activism: op.cit.* p.89.

64. Cronbach, Lee J., (1961). *Educational Psychology*, (London: Stapler Press), p.420.

65. Karani R.N., "Leadership For Democracy". In *the Nature of Leadership—A Practical Approach*, (ed.), Airan J.W., *op.cit.* p.38.

66. J. Filella, S.J., *'The Psychology of Leadership'*. In *The Nature of Leadership- A Pracitical Approach (ed)* Airan J.W., *op.cit.*, p.60.

67. Mishra, S.N., "Emerging Leadership in Rural India—A Case Study". In *Quarterly Journal of the Local Self-Government Institutions.*
    Pradipto Roy and Sèn, L.K., *Awareness of Community Development in Village India, Preliminary Report*, (Hyderabad: National Institute of Community Development, 1966).

68. Charles P. Loomis,"Change in Rural India as related to social power and sex" *Behavioural Sciences and Community Development, op.cit. p.4*.

69. (i) Abida Samiuddin, "The Emerging Pattern of Rural Leadership", *Kurukshetra*, (February 1977).

    (ii) Iqbal Narain, *et. al.* (1976). *The Rural Elite.* In *An Indian State— A Case Study in Rajasthan*, (Delhi: Manohar Book Service).

70. (i) Gupta L.C., "Changing Pattern of Rural Leadership—A Case Study", *Sociological Bulletin* 15, No.2 (Sept.1966) pp. 27-35.

    (ii) Pradipto Roy and Sen. L.K., *"Emerging Leadership'*. In *Awareness of Community Development in Village India-A Preliminary Report, op.cit.*

    (iii) Neeladri Raju K., "The Emerging Elite in Andhra Pradesh and Maharashtra and West Bengal", *Behavioural Sciences and Community Development*, Vol.5, No. 1, (March-1971).

71. (i) Inamdar N.A., "Functions of Village Panchayats, (Bombay: Popular Prakashan, (1970).

    (ii) Bada C.R., "The Study of Voting Behaviour in Gulbarga District" (Gulbarga. The Institute of Vichar Bharati Adyayana Vedike, 1974).

(iii) Ranga Rao K., "Rural Leadership and Conflict—A Study of an Andhra Village", *Economic and Political Weekly*, Vol.III, No.17, (April-1968).

72. Bada, C. R., *"Village Panchayat Key Leadership Pattern", Interdiscipline, op.cit.*

73. (i) *Ibid.*

(ii) Muthayya B.C., Neeladri Raju K., "Personal and Social Background of Elected Village Leaders", *Community Development and Panchayat Raj Digest*, Vol.4, No.3 (January 1973).

74. Jadeja Y.D., "Trends in Village Leadership in three villages of Gujarat", *Khadigramodyog*, 10, No.9, (June-1964), pp. 630-36.

75. (i) Bhatt K.S., *Panchayat Raj in Mysore*, (Unpublished Ph.D. thesis), (Bombay. University of Bombay, 1966).

(ii) Bhatt, K. S., "Emerging Pattern of Leadership in Panchayat Raj Set-up in Mysore State", Jacob, George ed., *Readings on Panchayat Raj* (Hyderabad. N.I.C.D., 1971).

(iii) Kariupurath, Paul, "The Emerging Pattern of Leadership in Mysore State", (Mysore. Administrative Training Institute).

76. (i) Bachenheimer, R., *"Elements of Leadership in an Andhra Village"*. In Park and Tinker (ed) *Leadership and Politcal Institutions in India, op.cit.*, pp. 445-52.

(ii) Harper, Edward B. and Louis G. Harper, "Political Organization and Leadership in a Karnataka Village" in *op.cit.*, pp. 453-69.

77. Abraham M.F.. *The Dynamics of Leadership in Village India,op.cit.*

78. Malla Reddy M.. *A Study on Few Socio-Psychological Correlates of student activism",op.cit.*

79. Abraham M.F. *op.cit.*

80. Pradipto Roy, *"Emerging Pattern of Rural Leadership"*. In Vidyarthi L.P. (ed) *Leadership in India, op.cit.*

81. Sen and Lalit K. and Roy P., *Awareness of Community Development in Village India, op.cit.*

82. Fliegel Frederick C., *et al, Agricultural Innovations in Indian Villages, op.cit.*

83. Dasgupta S., "Patterns of Agricultural Leadership and Innovations in Six Indian Villages", *Indian Journal of Extension Education*, Vol. 1 (4), (1968).

84. Sen, Lalit K., *Opinion Leadership in India—A Study of Inter-personal Communication in Eight Villages*, (Hyderabad. NICD, 1969).

85. Nirmalakanti Saha, "Leadership and Adoption of Agricultural Innovations", *Kurukshetra* (Jan. 1,1975), p.15.

86. Muthayya, "Psycho-Social Study of Panchayat Leaders in Tamil Nadu", Research Project at NICD, Hyderabad.

4

SAMPLE OF THE RURAL COMMUNITY WHERE THE STUDY WAS UNDERTAKEN: AREA OF STUDY AND SELECTION OF VILLAGES

The rural villages where the present study was conducted were drawn from five districts of the Telangana region of the State of Andhra Pradesh.

As the present research was designed to study the pattern of rural leadership in terms of their socio-psychological correlates the investigator wanted to involve a large number of rural leaders in her sample spread over a wide geographical area of the Telangana region. In order to examine their levels of aspirations, exposure to mass media, social awareness and democratic vs. authoritarian attitude, it was considered desirable to select those districts which were relatively progressive in terms of the educational attainment of people. Therefore, districts with high percentage of literacy level were selected for the purpose.

Sampling Design

Considering the nature and the objectives of the present research it was decided to adopt multistage purposive sampling technique. Under this procedure, as a first step, five districts were selected and from each district one of the blocks which was relatively progressive was chosen. A list of villages in all the blocks was obtained from the concerned block offices along with the details of population.

For the identification of villages, the following criteria were followed:

(a) literacy rate of population,

(b) population size of the villages ranging from 1500 to 3000 population;

(c) location of the villages within the radius of fifteen kilometres from the block headquaters;

(d) villages having multi-caste and class division;

(e) villages which have transportation, communication, and mass-media facilities.

Keeping the above criteria in view, the investigator, accompanied by a few post-graduate students of the department, visited the headquarters of the taluqs situated in the five districts of Telangana area. After a detailed discussion with the block development officials of the concerning blocks, six villages from each block were selected.

As the purpose of the investigator was to select the villages on the basis of the above mentioned criteria it was not possible to adopt random sampling procedure in this study. Therefore, the investigator was left with no alternative but to adopt "Multi-stage Purposive Sampling Technique"[1] which was equally scientific and relevant to the present study.

Identification of Leaders

After the identification of villages, the problem was to identify leaders from each village. A review of past researches in Indian rural leadership showed a lack of variability in methodology and approach.[2] The earlier studies focused on participant observation whereas the later studies laid heavily on the sociometric measure for the identification of leaders[3].

For the identification of leaders, studies on community leadership have used one of the following three techniques: (1) the positional approach, (2) the reputational approach and (3) the action or decisional approach.

In some cases a combination or modification of these three were also used.[4]

Until Hunter's study the positional approach was commonly employed to identify leaders.[5] The positional approach assumes that an idividual's power is closely correlated with his position in an official or semi-official hierarchy.[6] This method searches for the "potential power official hierarchy in the Community's institutionalized economic, political and civic structures.[7] The assumption is posited that those who hold vital positions in the community are also the key decision-makers in community action.

Investigators in the past regarded formal position as only one of the many possible factors in determining the individual's potential for affecting the behaviour of others. They have also reported that there were many power holders in our rural communities, who did not formally hold office in the major institutions and associations. The revelation that some of the important decisions of the community were taken outside the official positions shifted the focus of the investigators to the reputational and decisional approaches,

Currently, the most commonly used approach and consequently the one subjected to the most penetrating examination and criticism is the reputational approach.[8] The procedure is to "determine community power structures on the basis of judgements by community members who are considered 'knowledgeable' about community life. These 'judges' select names from lists of potential candidates based on imputed degrees of influence. Those persons, most frequently selected according to the given criteria, are said to constitute the power structure.[9] The reputation measure is an index of power attribution rather than of power expression.[10]

Most of these power-reputation or power-attribution studies stem from the work of Floyd Hunter in Regional City.[11] Since then, however, many studies have employed reputational approach in spite of the criticism it is facing.

This approach has been criticised for some shortcomings. The first criticism refers to the adequacy and validity of reputation as an index of the distribution of power.[12] A second point of debate is with regard to the 'monolithic power structure'.[13] Many have contended that there exist probably many pyramids of power rather than only one as the reputational approach may imply.[14] The difficulties involved in data collection and analysis are certain other disadvantages associated with this approach.[15]

Despite many shortcomings it is still widely used as this is one of the most rational approaches for indentification of such category of leaders.[16] In this process the villagers are asked to name a person or persons who can take initiative and carry on a programme and provide guidance and direction when they are involved in a problem. The questions framed to collect the opinions of the people are based either on their experiences of the past event and the role of the leader or on the possible behaviour of leaders in a given hypothetical situation. Thus the actual role played by a leader in a specific situation or event in the past or his psychological pre-disposition to play as perceived by the villagers in relation to an hypothetical situation, form the criteria for the identification of leaders through this approach.

An individual may be considered or recognized as a leader by virtue of the fact that the local residents recognise and acknowledge him to be one.[17] The respondents may be a selected panel or a population sample.[18] The list of leaders is prepared by the number of mentions each person receives as an index of recognition.[19] The final list of the leaders usually consists either of those individuals who have received the greatest number of mentions or of all leaders whose average ranking is above a certain arbitrarily set limit.[20] The third approach to the study of community power to be examined is the decision-making or issue-analysis approach. In the sociological literature, the decision-making approach has been referred to by different terms, such as 'event analysis'[21], 'issue approach',[22] 'action approach'.[23] It is some time considered to be an elaboration of the reputational method.[24] However, the critics of the reputational method are prone to propose the decision-making approach as the most direct and realistic approach to the study of community leadership.[25]

The action of leaders in decision-making on specific issues or events is taken as the criterion to identify leaders. A major advantage of this method is that it enables the researcher to measure power directly from the concrete observable behaviour of the participants in community actions,

The question may, however, be raised whether the action method essentially measures, or also measures, what the other techniques (i.e. reputational and positional method) propose to measure. There are serveral limitations inherent in this approach. Studies with this approach have been criticised on several grounds. First, none of the studies has considered the full range of issues that confront a decison-maker. Second, as noted by Peter Rossi[26] one can expect that most issues taken up for decision are settled without becoming controversies and hence difficult to perceive the psychological make-up of the leader. In view of the above decision-making approach, as a single method to measure leadership, is considered inadequate by several writers.

For the study of community leadership no single approach was found to be adequate. A combination of methods (any two or all three) appears to be the most satisfactory means for an adequate analysis of community leadership.

Combination of these three methods has been adopted by some researchers. Gupta[27] for example, employed "reputational and decisional"* approaches, Singh[28] *used a combination of "reputational" and "positional" methods, while Sen and Roy[29] depended upon "positional" and "sociometric" methods.

In their attempts to evolve a rational criterion for the identification of leaders there seems to be a growing consensus among investigators in the field for the synthesis of approaches as opposed to unitary approach.[30]

By analysing the three approaches, the investigator found that the positional and reputational approaches were most meaningful and reliable. In the present study, therefore, the positional and reputational approaches were used to select the formal and informal leaders, respectively.

All the elected members occupying certain positions in the village panchyats, including the Sarpanchas of the villages, were taken as formal leaders.

This study, though intended to cover all the Pancyayat members of 30 villages, the investigator could cover only 288 of them as the other members were not available at the time of the investigator's visit to the Panchayats. Informal leaders were selected through reputational method. While collecting the preliminary data about the informal leaders, 20 to 30 household heads were selected in each village at random depending on the size of the village. They were asked to nominate persons who took initiative in a variety of activities (Polymorphic) such as organising cultural programmes, sports, youth clubs, expressing their commitment and taking initiative in the developmental programmes of the villages, fighting for righteousness forgetting their personal interest, organizing movements like youth movements, social movements, for uplift of the oppressed, labour movements, co-operative movements, organizing activities to mobilize people for a collective redressal of their grievances, showing altruistic concern helping and guiding people in decision-making with regard to problems like electing a person to a given office, taking up new ventures, adopting a new innovation, *i.e.* all such activities as are concerned with the village and have socio-cultural bearing on the masses.

Out of the large number of leaders who were indentified through this approach only such persons as were perceived as leaders at least by 10 community members were included in the sample. Thus involving the comprehensive approach of multi-stage purposive sampling technique. 214 informal leaders, 288 formal leaders were identified from 30 villages.

TABLE 4.1

Table showing the literacy rate of the Districts of Telangana region as per Andhra Pradesh Samagra Darshan (1978)

Sl. No.	*District of Telangana Region*	*Literacy %*
* 1.	Hyderabad	40.37
* 2.	Khammam	18.51
* 3.	Warangal	18.11
* 4.	Nizamabad	17.19
* 5.	Nalgonda	17.05
6.	Medak	16.10
7.	Mahaboobnagar	15.55
8.	Karimnagar	15.31
9.	Adilabad	14.15

Source : 1971 Census.

* *Districts selected for study:*
Districts which were relatively progressive in the educational attainment of people, were selected for the purpose of study

TABLE 4.2

Table showing the Leaders of Five Districts classified by Informal and Formal Leadership

District	*Formal Leaders*	*Informal Leaders*	*Total*
District 1	61	44	105
District 2	57	44	101
District 3	59	46	105
District 4	56	42	98
District 5	55	38	93
Total (of all five Districts)	288	214	502

All the elected members occupying certain positions in village Panchayats, including the Sarpanches of the village were taken as formal leaders. While informal leaders as discussed earlier, were selected through reputational method.

TABLE 4.3

Table showing the sex-wise distribution of Formal and Informal Leaders

Sex	*Formal Leaders*	*Informal Leaders*	*Total*
Male	259	204	463
Female	29	10	39
Total	288	214	502

The above table reveals that in a total of 502 leaders, we have only 39 female leaders. This shows that even today women in India, particularly in villages occupy traditional roles and only in few cases they have come forward to take up the role of leadership. There are 29 formal leaders, who are elected to Panchayat institutions, whereas the informal leadership structure is concerned there are only 10 female leaders. This difference might be due to the reservation of seats for women in Panchayat institutions. In the present context even the small number of female leaders may be considered important (and further investigated) as an index of some change that might be taking place in rural India with regard to the status of women in social, cultural and political spheres.

Notes and References

1. This method was adopted by several investigators in their studies. For example:
   (i) N. Y. Reddy "Adolescent Adjustment in Relation to Home Environment", Unpublished Ph.D. thesis submitted to the Osmania University in 1966.
   (ii) K. R. Reddy, "Value Pattern and Vocational Sense Among High School Students", Unpublished Ph.D. thesis submitted to Osmania University in 1971.
   (iii) M. Malla Reddy, "A few Selected Socio-Psychological Correlates of Student Activism", Unpublished Ph.D. thesis submitted to Osmania University in 1973.
2. Udai Pareek and S.K. Reddy, (1966). *Studies in Indian Rural Leadership—A Review of Studies in Rural Leadership,* (ed) Udai Pareek (Delhi. Behavioural Science Centre,), pp 101-12.

3. (i) Oscar Lewis, "Group Dynamics in a North Indian Village": *A Study of Factions;* (New Delhi. Programme Evaluation Organization, Planning Commission, 1954).

   (ii) H.S. Dhillon, *"Leadership and Groups in a South Indian Village,"* (Delhi: Planning Commission, Programme Evaluation, Organization, 1954-55).

   (iii) S.N. Singh, *et, al. "Different types of Local Leadership in North Indian Villages."* In *Studies in Rural Leadership*, ed. Udai Pareek, *op.cit.*, pp. 1-11.

4. Charles M. Bonjian and David M. Oslon, "Community Leadership, Directions of Research", *Administrative Science Quarterly*. Vol.9, No.3 (October, 1964), p.280. They have discussed the shortcomings of each of the three approaches.

5. Floyd Hunter, *Community Power Structure: A Study of Decision . Makers*, (Chapel Hill: University of North Carolina Press,1953).

6. Robert A. Dahl, *Modern Political Analysis*, (Engle Wood Cliffs, New Jersey: Prentice-Hall, 1963), pp. 52-53.

7. Howard J. Ehrilich, *"Power and Democracy, A Critical Discussion"*. In *Power and Democracy in America*, eds. William V.D. Antonio and Howard J. Ehrlick (Notre Dame, Indiana University of Notre Dame Press, 1961), p. 99.

8. Charles M. Bonjean and David M. Oslon, "Community Leadership" *op.cit.*, p. 284.

9. Fisher S., "Community Power Studies: A Critique", *Social Research*, Vol. 29, No. 4, (Winter-1962), pp. 449-56.

10. Howard J. Ehrilich, "The Reputational Approach to the Study of Community Power", *American Sociological Review*, Vol.26, (December-1961), p. 926.

11. Floyed Hunter, 'Community Power Structure", *op.cit*.

12. Raymond E. Wolfinger, "Reputation and Reality in the Study of Community Power", *American Sociological Review*, Vol. XXV (October,1960), pp. 636-44.

13. Ernest A.T. Barth and Stuart D. Johnson, "Community Power and a Typology of Social Issues", *Social Forces*, Vol.38, (October, 1959), pp. 29-32.

14. William, H. Form and William, V.D. Antonio, "Integration and Cleavage Among Community Influentials in Two Border Cities", *American Sociological Review*, Vol.25 (December, 1959), pp. 804-14.

15. Raymond E. Wolfinger, "Reputation and Reality in the Study of Community Power". *op.cit*.

16. Avtar Singh, (1973). *Leadership Pattern and Village Structure. A Study of Six Indian Villages*, (New Delhi: Sterling Publishers Pvt. Ltd.),p.19.

17. William H. Form and Wanen L. Sanes, "Organized Labour`s Image of Community Power Structure", *Social Forces*, Vol. 38, (May, 1966), pp.332-341.

18. Robert E. Agger and Daniel Goldrich, "Community Power Structures and Partisanship", *American Sociological Review*, Vol. 23, (August, 1958), pp.383-92.

19. Delbert C. Miller, "Industry and Community Power Structure—A Comparative Study of an American and an English City", *American Sociological Review*, Vol. 23, (February, 1958), pp.9-15.

20. Among the Studies that have used the Reputational Method exclusively are: B.N. Sahay, "Village Leaders and Development Programmes", *Khadigramodyog*, 13, No.7, (April, 1967), pp. 510-15, Harjinder Singh, "Community Leadership—An Analysis", *Adivasi*, No.2 (1966), pp. 25-30.
21. Solon T. Kimball and Marion Pearsall, "Event Analysis as an Approach to Community Study", *Social Forces*, Vol. 34, (October, 1955), pp. 58-63.
22. Robert. A. Dahl, "A Critique of the Ruling Elite Model", *American Political Science Review:* Vol.52, (June, 1958), pp. 463-69.
23. Avatar Singh, *Leadership Pattern and Village Structure*, *op.cit*. pp.11-14.
24. Robert Presthees, *Men at the Top: A Study in Community Power*, (New York: Oxford University Press, 1964).
25. Linton C. Freeman, *et.al.*, "Locating Leaders in Local Communities —A Comparison of Some Alternative Approaches", *American Sociological Review*, Vol, 28 (October, 1963). pp. 791-98.
26. Peter H. Rossi, "Community Decision Making", *Administrative Science Quarterly*, Vol. 1 (March, 1957), pp.438-39.
27. Raghu Raj Gupta, (1966). *Decision Makers on a Gramdan Village*, (Lucknow, Planning Research and Action Institute.).
    * He used 'Reputational-Decisional' method to know about decision makers who were most influential and powerful in making six important decisions in a village in Uttar Pradesh.
28. Harjinder Singh, (1968). *Village Leadership—A Case Study of Village Mohali in Punjab*, (Jalandhar. Sterling Publishers).
    * Singh used reputational method to identify persons who would exert most influence in various aspects of Community life. Through positional approach, he defined persons as leaders, who occupied elective or appointive offices in the community.
29. Lalit K. Sen and Prodipto Roy, "The Emerging Leadership". In *Awaremess of Community Development in Village India, Preliminary Report* (Hyderabad. N.I.C.D. 1966), pp. 42-48.
30. (i) For critical review of various methods See: C.M. Bongean and David M. Olson, "Community Leadership", Perspectives on the American Community, (ed.) Ronald L. Warren (Chicago: Rand McNally and Co., 1966), pp.499-512.
    (ii) Tarry N. Clark ed. *Community Structure and Decision Making: Comparative Analysis* (San Francisco. Chandler Publishing Co., 1968), pp. 72-81.

5

DEVELOPMENT 0F TOOLS

As discussed earlier, the présent investigation is designed to examine a number of hypotheses formulated under the conceptual framework of this study. This necessitated the development of more than one tool, depending on the variable concerned. The procedure adopted for the development of tools and the measurement of each of these variables is discussed individually and in detail in the present chapter.

Measurement of Democratic vs. Authoritarian Leadership

Democratic vs. authoritarian behaviour is the major response-variable in the present investigation. Investigators in the field have employed different tools or indices for identiftying the leader's behaviour. Some investigators in the field have employed interview techniques[1] and observed the leaders' behaviour in group situations. Some have conducted experiments[2] to study the leader's behaviour. The questionnaire technique has also been employed by certain other investigators.

Among the many alternatives, the tool adopted for this study was determined by the following considerations.

1. The intention of the investigator to study an extensive sample spread over a wide geographical area.

2. A method that could be applied over a short time with a view to gathering information within a relatively short period of time.

3. The Democratic attitutde was to be studied as a subjective predisposition rather than an actual observed behaviour.

4. The need to elicit responses which would be fairly concrete, permitting quantification and scoring, and also to make it meaningful and easy for the respondents.

After careful consideration and examination of the different possibilities, it was felt that a verbal situation test would meet better the demands of the investigator than most other types of instruments.

The verbal situation test has been employed by a number of investigators[3] to measure attitudes and pre-dispositions. Thus the choice fell on this technique.

At the outset, a large number of situations were constructed keeping in view the rural democratic processes in which the leaders are involved and where they express their reaction either positive or negative. After intensive consultations with a number of University teachers, educators, and research workers in psychology and education, fifty situations were constructed relating to the general rural socio-cultural situations. These situations were capable of evoking positive or negative response of the respondents depending on their psychological predisposition.

The preliminary draft was circulated among 36 senior and experienced researchers all over the country for their opinions and comments. These experts were requested to bear following points in mind while considering the suitability of each item.

1. Whether the item is likely to elicit the nature of behaviour (democratic or authoritarian) of the subject.

2. Whether the particular situation would be relevant and meaningful from the point of view of the respondents i.e. rural leaders.

The Opinions of the Experts Item No.6 Original Form

It is often said that the poor people are exploited by a few rich elders of the village. Do you think we should:

1. accept this to avoid conflict;

2. protest against such incidents;

3. bring a revolution to stop such practices.

This item was modified in the following way in the final form:

Item No.6

Suppose you have been repeatedly told by your followers about the exploitation of poor by a few rich elders of the village, what would be your usual reaction?

1. Take it as normal in our society;

2. Try to educate such people for changing their ways of treating the employees;

3. Expose them.

The Scheme of Response

Apart from the content of the item, the most important question to be considered was the scheme of responses. Some situation tests employ the open response system where the respondents are allowed to give their own responses to be codified and quantified subsequently. But most of the situation tests furnish the respondent with fixed alternatives from which the respondent has to choose the one that most nearly approximates his own response. The open ended scheme while permitting the respondent greater freedom suffers from the disadvantages of putting a high premium on the verbal ability of the respondent and also subjectivity in codification and quantification. The fixed alternatives system, though suffers from a certain degree of arbitrariness, nevertheless has the advantage from the point of view of scoring and classification.

In view of this each item in the situation test was followed by three alternative responses signifying a different degree of democratic behaviour— low, moderate and high. These specific alternatives were also circulated to the experts alongwith the situations to elicit their judgements as to whether the alternatives in their opinion reflected the different degrees of democratic attitude. It was felt that a three point measurement would be adequate. The three-point scheme was felt to be free from other possible disadvantages involved in employing a five point or seven point scheme. All the same it was felt that it would provide a finer degree of differentiation than a two point scheme. The three-point scheme has been preferred by a number of investigators.

In the second preliminary form, 40 items were included. After finalising the items and the scheme of answering as stated above, it was decided to carry out a preliminary study with the following objectives:

(1) To find out the item validity so as to enable the elimination of those items which failed to discriminate between those who score high on the total test and those who score low on the total test.

(2) To establish the reliability of the test.

(3) To establish the validity of the test.

The preliminary form, consisting of 40 items, was administered to a representative sample of 120 leaders drawn from different villages in the Telangana region. The distribution of the total score was as follows:

Range	*Frequency*
40 - 49	3
50 - 59	2
60 - 69	14
70 - 79	40
80 - 89	42
90 - 99	13
100 -109	5
110 -119	1
Total	120

It may be thus seen that the distribution is very nearly approximate to the normal distribution.

Item Validity

To carry out the item validity, the following procedure was adopted.

The highest quartile and the lowest quartile were selected as the high and the low groups and the average scores of the two groups on each item was worked out alongwith the standard deviation. 't' ratios were calculated for each item applying the formula[4] out of the 40 items, only 32

$$t = \frac{X_H - X_L}{\sqrt{\dfrac{(X_H - X_H)^2 + (X_L - X_L)^2}{n\,(n-1)}}}$$

items were found to be significant at 0.05 level as per 't' values. These 32 items were retained and the rest of the items were eliminated. Two more items were eliminated as they were check items (for details please refer Appendix-V).

Reliability of the Scale

For this purpose, 'test and retest reliability' procedure was adopted. A revised form of the scale including only thirty (30) items was administered to a group of 60 subjects. The test was administered to them again after an interval of 50 days. The scores of the 60 subjects on the two occasions were correlated. The correlation 'r' was found to be, 0.85. The value was high enough to be accepted.

Validity

For establishing the validity of the test, the concurrent validity method was adopted by using Ansari[5] value orientation scale which includes authoritarianism — non-authoritarianism dimensions.

The scores of the two scales on a sample of 60 subjects were obtained and coefficient of correlation between these two scores was computed. The obtained coefficient of correlation between the two scores was 0.68. This showed the high validity of the items of the test.

The Final Form

The final form, with the 30 items, was thus accepted for the final administration in view of the satisfactory reliability and validity measures obtained in the pilot study.

II. SOCIO-ECONOMIC STATUS SCALE

There have been a number of studies to identify the socio-economic status of the subjects of both rural and urban areas. Some of the investigations include Pandya[6], Sirisikar[7] Parmatma Saran,[8] Abraham[9] Patnaik,[10] Ghurye,[11] Bose[12] and Dube.[13] The last mentioned being carried out in this part of the country where the present investigation is undertaken. These investigators have adopted a variety of methods in studying the socio-economic status of the subjects.

There have been many scales in the field to measure the socio-economic status, developed by Pareek and Trivedi,[14] Kuppuswamy,[15] Radhudkar[16] Verma[17] of all the scales one developed by Pareek and Trivedi for rural subjects has been in common use in India. However, all the scales, including the one developed by Pareek are outdated and it was felt that they were unsuitable in this investigation as:

(1) Many changes have taken place in recent years in our society, which have altered the social structure of a rural society (occupational structure, economic relations, family relations, etc.,). The above scales are outdated and do not take into account these changes.

(2) The present investigator was interested in developing a 'socio-economic status scale'suitable to the rural population of Andhra Pradesh, especially for the Telangana area.

Therefore, for the purpose of the present study, a scale was developed which called for information with regard to the legally accepted caste (i.e. Scheduled Caste, Backward Caste, Foreward Caste), education, occupation, income, landholding, type of house, membership in different organizations of the respondents.

Earlier studies in relation to social stratification have suggested that caste, landed property, political power, education and occupation were important factors, especially with regard to rural areas. In the present study, besides caste, landed property, education and occupation, three more components were included. They are family income, type of house and social participation.

After finalising the dimensions in this scale, each dimension was further divided into different levels to identify the status of an individual in the given dimension in terms of these levels. The scoring and the weightages given to each level under each component of socio-economic status was decided in consultation with the officials in the Bureau of Economics and Statistics, three Taluk officials and three Revenue Inspectors. A weightage of zero to ten was given for education, one to ten for income, zero to nine for land and social participation, zero to six for type of house, one to six for occupation and one to three for caste background.

Reliability and Validity

Both reliability and validity of the scale were found out. For establishing the reliability of the scale, the test and retest method was adopted. The scale was administered twice to a sample of 60 leaders selected at random from different villages, with an interval of 50 days. The co-efficient of correlation of the two scores was 0.87 showing a high level of significance of the scale in terms of its reliability.

Inter- Judge Reliability

Two persons, quite independent of each other, interviewed a sample of 60 families of rural leaders selected at random from different villages. The rank order correlation obtained was 0.91 indicating high inter-judge reliability.

Validity

The content validity of the scale is borne out by a method of collecting information on each item. The concurrent validity was found to be very high when correlated with the scores obtained by using Pareek's scale on a sample of 60 leaders. The coefficient of correlation computed between the two measures was found to be 0.78. Thus the scale was found to be valid and reliable for employing on the sample involved in this study.

III. EXPOSURE TO MASS MEDIA AND EXTENSION AGENCY CONTACT

Exposure to mass media and extension agency contact is another variable for which a tool had to be constructed. As already pointed out, exposure to mass media and contact with extension agency are important in broadening the outlook and in developing democratic attitude among the leaders. Investigators like Saran,[18] Abraham,[19] Sirsikar[20] have studied the influence of media exposure as an important factor for the emergence of one as a leader in a rural community. Media exposure and extension agency contact was studied, by developing a structured questionnaire involving a number of questions on items like newspaper reading, radio listening, movie exposure, and respondent's contacts with rural development agents like extension officers, health visitors *etc*.. With a view to measuring the relative levels of exposure of the respondents, the responses were sought on a four point scale.

Thus, a scale was devised to study the levels of media exposure and extension agency contact. In constructing this scale, instruments adopted in earlier researches were taken as basis. 24 questions were prepared to elicit information on media exposure and extension agency contact. The items then were submitted to several experts in the field of education, psychology and sociology alongwith the other tools, seeking their suggestions for necessary modifications in the items in terms of their structure and content. On the basis of the opinion of the experts necessary alterations were made and seven items eliminated.

Scheme of Responses

Response alternatives were presented on a four point scale. Regularly, occasionally, very rarely and never were the four levels of exposure. The following weightages were given to the four levels of exposure.

Levels of Exposure	*Weightage given*
Regularly	3
Occasionally	2
Very rarely	1
Never	0

Total scores for a respondent could range from 45 to 0, with a high score indicating high degree of exposure to mass media and extension agency contact, and conversely, the low score reflecting a lower degree of exposure.

After finalising the items and the scheme of response, a preliminary study was carried out with the following objective:

1. To establish the reliability of the test.

Reliability

An attempt was made to establish the reliability of the scale by administering it a second time randomly to 60 leaders from different villages, with an interval of fifty days. The reliability coefficent of the two scores was calculated and was found to be 0.74. Thus the scale was found to be adequately reliable.

Validity

As the purpose of this tool was limited for collecting the information regarding the respondent's exposure to mass media and extension agency contacts, the items included in the interview schedule were simple and direct questions like:

1. How often do you read newspapers?
2. How often do you attend agricultural demonstration classes?
3. How often do you discuss with the village health visitors about health problems? *etc., etc.*

Therefore, the investigator accepted the test on the basis of its *a priori* validity and administered the interview schedule on the sample selected.

IV. MEASURING THE LEVELS OF ASPIRATIONS

Another tool required in this investigation was the tool to measure the levels of aspiration. Investigators working on levels of aspirations have employed a number of techniques. Laboratory studies have employed Rotters Aspiration Board. Another investigator employed portrait writing technique-"The person I like to be". Yet another technique employed is Cassells' level of aspiration test.[21] On this test the subject is asked to estimate the number of XS he could mark on a form sheet in a given time. The subject was then asked to make the XS in the given time. The scoring is done taking the discrepancy between the subjects' estimate and the actual number of times completed. This aspiration test is a goal discrepancy measure which also includes induced frustration. Another common technique employed especially in large scale quantitative investigations is the pictorial self auctioning ladder scale developed by Cantril[22]. This technique has the following advantages:

1. It is easy to administer even to unsophisticated subjects.

2. It is easy to employ in a large scale investigation, involving extensive samples.

3. The responses can easily be quantified.

Despite the inherent advantages the scale has its own drawbacks. The scale must be understood by the respondents by relating it to their daily life and situations. Respondents must have an understanding of the position on the scale and relating it to their present and future status.

Therefore, for the purpose of the present study close ended questions were developed to measure the expectations of the respondents towards education, income, and future leadership position (status). It was assumed that, with these questions, respondents will be in a position to understand the aspects to give correct answers. A weightage of zero to 10 was given for education, income and leadership status.

Reliability

An attempt was made to establish the reliability of the scale by administering it twice to a group of sixty leaders selected randomly from different villages, with an interval of fifty days. The reliability coefficient of the two scores was calculated and which came to 0.71. Thus the scale was found to be adequately reliable.

Validity

As the purpose of this tool was limited for collecting the information regarding the future expectations of the respondents' education, income and future leadership positions, the items included were simple and direct questions. Therefore, the investigator accepted the test on the basis of its *a priori* validity and administered the tool on the sample selected.

V. SCALE ON SOCIAL AWARENESS

In the present investigation, as discussed earlier, it was felt that it would be relevant to examine the levels of social awareness among the leaders with a view to finding out its relationship to their democratic attitude. The logic behind this idea is the fact that India is undergoing a process of modernization and the social behaviour and the democratic outlook of the leaders is an important factor in accelerating the process of social change from traditional to the modern pattern. In this connection it was assumed that leaders with progressive outlook, *i.e.* with high levels of social awareness would exhibit democratic behaviour. For this it was felt necessary to employ a scale to measure the levels of social awareness among the rural leaders.

Previously studies were undertaken to investigate the leaders' political awareness, and awareness of certain issues of the society. Those studies included information at cognitive level. Pradipto Roy and Lalit K. Sen[23] have studied awareness of community development among the leaders and massess. S.N. Mishra[24] has studied awareness of leaders about certain aspects of change.

In this study social awareness is not limited to cognitive level information about the existence of new institutions, and prevalence of changes, but it is conceived as "problem consciousness" implying a desire on the part of the leaders to overthrow traditional injustices and create a new social order. Social awareness is characterised by the following dimensions:

(a) their knowledge about the existence of the new institutions and changes,

(b) their attitude towards the desirability of these changes and new institutions,

(c) their feeling regarding the possibility of attaining these changes.

So far no standard scale is available to measure this variable. So it was considered a significant contribution to the field of rural education if a new tool was constructed to measure the social awareness based on the operational definition of the concept.

A number of items covering the information on new institutions and dominant themes of socio-economic and political changes were prepared. The following areas of changing rural culture and institutions have been included in the development of the present scale.

1. Cooperative institutions,

2. Educational institutions,

3. Adult franchise,

4. Untouchability,

5. Caste,

6. Child marriages,

7. Child labour,

8. Female descendancy,

9. Divorce,

10. Superstitions,

11. Social equality,

12. Owner-tenant relationship in agriculture,

13. Agriculture labour-unions,

14. Self-employment schemes,

15. Family Planning,

16. Modern medical practices,

17. Dowry system and

18. Employer-employees relationship.

The tool was developed covering eighteen broad socio-cultural themes and institutions in which planned changes have been introduced. In order to examine the reactions of the rural leaders towards such changes, three dimensional questions covering each theme were prepared. Each broad question comprised three sub-question items: (1) cognitive awareness, (2) desirability of change and (3) possibility of change as perceived by the respondents.

Reactions of the respondents on each sub-question item under each broad question were sought on a three point scale and, therefore, altogether nine responses were collected on each question. Depending on the nature of responses and the score on the scale, the respondents were arranged on a continuum from higher levels of awareness to lower levels of awareness.

The statements prepared were in two directions — positive and negative.

Positive Statements

Here score values of 1, 2, 3, were assigned to the three alternatives—disagree, undecided and agree.

Negative Statements

Here the scheme of scoring was reversed. The dis-agreement with the statements has higher score and shows an acceptance of change and modern outlook. So the score value of 3, 2, 1 were assigned to the three alternatives—disagree, undecided, and agree.

Thus a higher score on the total scale would indicate a higher degree of change prone outlook (social awareness).

Preliminary Draft of the Scale

The preliminary draft of the scale comprising 25 broad questions and three sub-question items under each broad question was prepared. This form was circulated to a number of experts in the field of education, sociology and psychology, inviting their suggestions for the improvement of the scale in terms of the content and composition of the questions. Necessary modifications were made following their comments and judgments. The revised form with 23 broad questions with three sub-question items under each broad question was prepared. After finalising the structure of each item included in the tool, it was decided to carry out the preliminary study with the following objectives.

(1) To carry out an item validity to enable the elimination of those items which fail to discriminate between those who score high and on the total test and those who score low on total test.

(2) To establish the reliability of the test.

(3) To establish the validity of the test.

The scale was then administered to a sample for 120 leaders drawn from different villages of Telangana region. The distribution of the scores was as follows:

Range	Frequency
76 - 85	1
86 - 95	2
96 - 105	1
106 - 115	5
116 - 125	14
126 - 135	13
136 - 145	31
146 - 155	14

156 - 165	13
166 - 175	10
176 - 185	8
186 - 195	5
196 - 205	3
Total	120

Analysis

The scores were worked out by summation method for each individual on total scale. Then 25 per cent of the subjects with highest total scores and 25 per cent of the subjects with lowest total scores were chosen to constitute the high group and low group respectively. Mean value, standard deviation and standard error were computed for the two groups. Critical ratios were worked out to find out the significance of difference between the mean scores of the high and low groups.

Depending on the critical ratios only those items that were found to reveal mean differences at least at 0.5 level of significance were considered for retaining in the second preliminary form. Thus 20 broad items were approved on this basis. Two items were further dropped out for reasons of vagueness and duplication of items. Thus the second preliminary form had 18 broad questions.

1. Reliability of the Test

The test and retest reliability procedure was adopted for establishing the reliability of the test. The revised form of the test including 18 broad socio-cultural questions, was administered to a group of 60 leaders drawn from the previous sample. The test was administered to the sample again after an interval of 50 days. The co-efficient of correlation of the two scores was 0.82. This indicated the high reliability of the scale.

2. Validity of the Test

For the purpose of establishing the validity of the scale it was decided to work out the concurrent validity by using, the 'Value Orientation' scale of Malla Reddy[25] which included items on socio-economic and political changes in terms of traditionalism and modernism. The coefficient of correlation computed on the scores of the two scales administered to a sample of 60 subjects was found to be 0.81. This pointed out the high validity of the scale.

3. The Final Form

Thus a final form of the tool covering 18 socio-cultural themes was accepted after establishing its validity and reliability as explained above. The same was used to measure the 'social awareness' of the subjects in this study.

Notes and References

1. Ralph, M. Stogdill, Carroll, L. Shartle, Robert J. Wherry and William E. Jaynes, "A Factorial Study of Administrative Behaviour". In Browne, C.G. and Cohn, Thomas, (ed.), *The Study of Leadership*, (Illinois. The Interstate Printers and Publishers, 1958), pp.3 57-66.
2. (i) Ronald, Lippitt. *An Experimental Study of Authoritarian and Democratic Group Atmospheres*. (University of Iowa Studies for Child Welfare, 1939), 16. No.3.
   (ii) Ronald, Lippitt, Ralph, K. White, Kurt Lewin, "Pattern of Aggressive Behaviour in Experimentally Created Social Climate". In Hemphill, J.K., and Coons, A.E. *Leader Behaviour Description*, (Columbus, Ohio, Personnel Research Board, The Ohio State University, 1950).
3. G.W. and F.H. All Port, "The Allport—A-S Reaction Study", Houghton Mifflin Co., 1928-39, cited from *Theory and Practice of Psychologcal Testing*, by Frank S. Freeman, (New York. Holt Reinehart and Winston, Inc., 1960), p.468.
4. Allen L. Edwards. *Technique of Attitude Scale Construction* (Vakils, Feffer and Simons Pvt. Ltd., Hague Building, 9 Sprott Road, Ballard Estate, Bombay, 1969), p. 153.
5. A. Ansari, 'Value Orientation Scale", Department of Psychology, Aligarh Muslim University, given in *Handbook of Psychological and Sociological Instruments* (ed.), Pareek and Venkateswara Rao, (Ahmedabad : Sahitya Mudranalaya), pp. 290-93.
6. Pandya, B.B. 'Occupational Patterns of Scheduled Caste in Ahmedabad District" *J.Gujarat, Res. Society, 19(2)*, pp.112-24.
7. V.M. Sirsikar. *Elite in Developing Society, op.cit.*,pp. 38-59.
8. Paramatma Saran. *Rural Leadership in the Context of India's Mdernization*, (New Delhi. Vikas Publishing House, Pvt. Ltd. 1978), pp. 54-59.
9. F. Abraham. *Dynamics of Leadership in Rural India*, (Allahabad, India International Publication, 1976), pp. 45-50.

10. Patnaik N., "Caste and Occupation in Rural Policy," -*Man in India*, 34, pp. 257-70.

11. Ghurye, G.S.. *Caste Class and Occupation*, (Bombay. Popular Book Depot), p. 335.

12. Bose, A.B. and Malhotra, S.P., "Some Characters of Occupational Castes in Central, Lower, Luni in Western Rajasthan", *Eastern Anthropologist*, 17, pp,. 137-56.

13. Dube, S.C. "Ranking of Castes in Telangana Villages", *Eastern Anthropologist*, 8(324), pp. 182-90.

14. Pareek U. and Trivedi G., "Reliability and Validity of a Rural Socio-Economic Status Scale", *op. cit.* pp. 34-40.

15. Kuppuswami B., "A Scale to Measure Socio-Economic Status", *op.cit.*, pp. 1-10.

16. Radhukar, W.D., "A Scale for Measuring Socio-Economic Status of Indian Farm Families", *Nagpur Agriculture College Magazine*, 34, pp. 30-33.

17. Verma, R. M. 'Development of a Tool to Appraise Socio-Economic Status", *J. Psychol. Res.* pp. 35-39.

18. Saran P., *Rural Leadership in the Context of India's Modernization, op.cit.*, pp. 94-103.

19. Abraham F.. *Dynamics of Leadership in Village India, op.cit.*, pp. 56-58.

20. Sirsikar V.M., *Elite in Developing Society, op.cit.*

21. Cassels's Level of Aspiration Test, cited in S.B. Red J.L. McCary, Bette, Johnson, "A Study of Relationship between Aspiration Levels and Academic Achievements", *The Journal of Education Research*, Vol. 55, No. 4, (December-January 1962) pp. 159-63.

22. (i) Kilpatrick, F.P. and H. Cantril, "Self-anchoring scaling: A measure of individual's Unique reality worlds", *Journal of Individual Psychology*, 1960, 16 (2).

    (ii) Hadley Cantril, (1965) *"The Pattern of Human Concerns,"* (New Brunswick, N.J. Rutgers University Press,). Chap.3.

23. Pradipto Roy and Lalit K. Sen, *Awareness of Community Development in Rural India*, A Preliminary Report, *op.cit.*

24. S. N. Mishra, "Emerging Leadership in Rural India, A Case Study", *Quarterly Journal of the Local Self Government Institute*, Vol.XVII, No.2 (Oct. Dec. 1976), pp. 187-207.

25. M. Malla Reddy, "Scale on Value Orientation". In *A Few Selected Socio-Psychological Correlates of Student Activism, op.cit.*

6

DATA ANALYSIS AND RESULTS

As already stated the major objectives of this study are:

(1) to know the socio-economic background of the leaders, with a view to examining whether the leadership is the privilege of certain sections of the village community.

(2) to investigate the relationship between the socio-economic status of the rural leaders and their democratic vs. authoritarian attitude.

(3) to estimate the degree of exposure of the rural leaders to mass media and extension-agencies and its influences on their democratic vs. authoritarian attitude.

(4) to find out the levels of aspirations of rural leaders and their relation to their democratic vs. authoritarian attitude.

(5) to measure the degree of social awareness of the rural India leaders and its influence on their democratic vs. authoritarian attitude.

The previous chapter discussed the research procedures adopted, the criteria for the selection of each independent variable, the operational definitions evolved for each variable, and the hypotheses formulated in the study. The techniques employed in the development of the tools and the sampling design were also discussed. The present chapter mainly concerns with the analysis of the data and the discussion of the findings.

While presenting the results here it is considered desirable to recall the hypotheses presented and the rationale discussed in the chapters. Therefore, in the prefatorial statements of each section, a discussion of the rationale for each hypothesis is elaborated with further arguments. Thus, the present chapter is devoted to a discussion of the rationale for each hypotheses, the analysis and interpretation of the data.

For this purpose the chapter is divided into four sections. The data and the results of the study are presented separately in different sections as shown below:

Section-I : Socio-economic background and the democratic vs. authoritarian attitude of rural leaders.

Section-II : Exposure to mass media and extension-agency contacts and democratic vs. authoritarian attitude of rural leaders.

Section-III : Levels of aspirations and democratic vs. authoritarian attitude of rural leaders.

Section-IV : Social awareness and democratic vs. authoritarian attitude of rural leaders.

As already described, democratic vs. authoritarian attitude of the rural leaders was measured through a verbal situation test administered to 502 subjects. The frequency distribution of democratic vs. authoritarian attitude scores of the entire sample is given as follows:

Class Interval		*Frequency*
32 - 38		2
39 - 45		17
46 - 52		34
53 - 59		36
60 - 66		67
67 - 73		184
74 - 80		130
81 - 87		32
	Total	502

Mean : 68.306 Median : 70.11
Standard Deviation: 10.035. Range: 32-87

For testing the hypotheses, correlational analysis was done by computing the coefficients of correlation between democratic vs. authoritarian attitude on one hand and socio-economic status, levels of exposure to mass-media and extension-agency contact, levels of aspiration and degree of social awareness on the other.

SECTION I

SOCIO-ECONOMIC STATUS AND DEMOCRATIC VS. AUTHORITARIAN ATTITUDE

A general observation of leadership pattern in the Indian rural communities suggests that the leadership role is often associated with dominant caste groups based on an authoritarian structure built around ascriptive methods of transfer of power. The leadership phenomenon in India has always been context bound defined by the socio-cultural conditions. Obviously, the cultural themes of the Indian community like 'hierarchy', 'pluralism', 'family and kinship loyalities' were some of the factors determining power structure and leadership role of the different segments of Indian community. This being so, the leadership was not opened to all groups, the sources of leadership were thus closed and predetermined.[1]

India, in view of its commitment to the principle of equality has undertaken several programmes to establish an egalitarian social order. Many opportunities have been created for the people with merit and achievement to participate in decision making and to take up leadership role. The relationship between the socio-economic status and the leadership role, therefore, needs to be understood in the context of our shifting emphasis on the achieved status rather than the ascribed status.

While all the democratic countries believe in the "achieving society"[2] not many studies have been undertaken to see whether these democratic attitudes were really present in all society though they were theoretically assumed to be present. The earlier conclusions of sociologists that the achieved status was a characteristic of the highly developed countries rather than the less developed countries, was based on simplistic analysis of rural realities. It is desirable that such explanations emerge on the basis of empirical researches designed for different types of societies which are at different levels of transition from traditional to modern.

It is logical to presume that the new forces must be causing changes in the composition of the rural leadership in view of our emphasis to break away from the tradition and to move towards rationality and efficiency: the hallmarks of modernity. In support of this assumption, some studies indicate that the leadership in rural India is becoming more and more democratic[3] as the traditionally privileged and dominant groups are increasingly replaced by the active and achievement-oriented population, who are dynamic, dominant and can take initiative in the rural community.[4]

It is understandable that the people who had no say in the selection of leaders in the earlier context of our closed society, today no more accept the privileges of the dominant groups with regard to the leadership role[5]. The system of universal adult franchise involving the principles of democracy for the election of leaders, decentralisation of administration to make people self-reliant, have contributed to democratic outlook among the people. This outlook appears to be reinforced through many educational opportunities both formal and non-formal, particularly among the higher to deprived classes of the society, to enable them to compete with the privileged groups[6].

However, it would be a simplistic observation to say that the traditional determinants of power structure like higher caste status, economic position do not act as intervening variables, influencing the leadership pattern though the pattern of leadership under the present context has undergone considerable transformation from the past. But the extent to which the socio-cultural factors still operate as powerful variables with regard to leadership pattern and what is the nature and composition of the present leadership in the Indian community are some of the issues which call for an empirical investigation.

The present study, therefore, is an attempt to examine the social background of the leaders and see whether the leadership pattern is still associated with the privileged social background of the people. Based on this conceptual framework, a scale was developed in the present study to measure the socio-economic status of the leaders. The scale is a composite index of caste background, educational level, income, occupations, extent of land ownings, type of house and level of social participation of the respondents. The scale was administered on a sample of 502 subjects. The frequency distribution of the scores of 502 respondents on socio-economic status scale is given below.

Class Interval	*Frequency*
11 - 16	14
17 - 22	97
23 - 28	270
29 - 34	101
35 - 40	14
41 - 46	6
Total	502

Mean: 26.308 Standard Deviation: 4.99

The perusal of the above data reveal that while majority of rural leaders hails from middle socio-economic background, a significant representation of such leaders is noted from the lower strata of the society also.

As stated earlier, it was also the concern of the present study to examine the relationship of such changing class background of rural leaders with their outlook towards democratic vs. authoritarian behaviour. In the earlier context of our society the very matter of recruitment of leaders was based on the authoritarian model and people with authoritarian background were the privileged in this regard.

Therefore, one can infer from such process that our earlier leaders were usually "authoritarian", whether this manifested in their actual behaviour or not. In the present context of social change, resulting in open recruitment of leaders from all levels of society, based on the principles of merit achievement, such leaders formal or informal, should have been psychologically predisposed in favour of the processes of democratization.

An examination of the democratic vs. authoritarian attitude of these leaders involving their class backgournd as a variable might reveal significant results of educational importance. Thus the following hypothesis was formulated.

Higher the level of socio-economic status of the respondents, greater is the degree of their democratic behaviour.

For testing the hypothesis, a correlational anaysis was undertaken by computing the coefficients of correlation between socio-economic status and democratic attitude of the different groups of respondents.

Correlational Analysis

Coefficients of correlation between the scores of respondents obtained on socio-economic status scale and democratic vs. authoritarian behaviour scale were worked out using the product moment method. The table below shows Pearson's Product Moment correlations between socio-economic status and democratic vs. authoritarian attitude computed for different samples.

TABLE 6.1

Table showing coefficients of correlation of socio-economic status and democratic vs. authoritarian attitude for total sample, and sub-groups within the sample.

Sample	*Number*	*Coefficient of correlation between Socio-Economic status and Authoritarian attitude*	*value*	*Levels of significance*
Total Sample	502	+ 0.23	5.40	0.05
Formal Leaders	288	+ 0.25	4.512	0.01
Informal Leaders	214	+ 0.16	2.342	0.05

The values of the correlations shown above are positive and significant at 0.05 level both in the total sample and informal leaders. However, in the case of the formal leaders, the correlation is significant only at 0.01 level, though it still maintains a positive relationship.

Discussion of the Findings

The findings of this study supported the hypothesis formulated by revealing a positive relationship between the socio-economic status and levels of democratic attitude. The coefficient of correlation both for formal and informal leaders worked out separately and presented in the table, is an indication of the fact that the overall relationship between socio-economic status and democratic behaviour in each case is significant with some variation.

As evidenced in this study there is a greater degree of positive relationship between socio-economic status and democratic behaviour in the case of formal leaders (r=0.25) in comparison with informal leaders (r = 0.16). Thus it may be concluded safely that the factor of formal and non-formal background of leaders does not produce any significant change in their democratic attitude.

It is interesting to note from the study that the earlier interwoven relationship between the class background and the power structure seems to have been shaken in changing India. While it is possible to offer a number of explanations for such changes in the power structure of our rural communities, the institutional changes with reference to Zamindari system, caste system, the village judicial system and the introduction of well delineated Panchayats system based on the elections may be considered some of the important factors contributing to this changing phenomenon. The adequate realisation of the masses about the earlier exploitation of the landlords, dominant caste groups, supported by legal reforms must have added to their strength in overthrowing the earlier domination of the privileged groups. Better educational facilities, occupational mobility, migration to urban communities, measures taken to uplift the down trodden must have enlightened the masses in the selection of their leaders.

There is positive relationship between the present composition of the rural leadership determined in terms of their changing class background and their attitude towards democratic vs. authoritarian style. It is gratifying to note that today's rural leader is democratic in his behaviour and can be considered as a "man" in the process of liberation. It is interesting to note that the findings of this study do not support the hypothetical explanations of Paulo Freire that "people in general who were yesterday's oppressed, emerge as today's oppressors". The findings of this study, which are not in congruence with the observation of Paulo Freire, therefore, need to be interpreted in terms of his thesis[7] on the resolution of the oppressor-oppressed contradiction. Paulo Freire observes that the moment the new regime harden into dominating "bureaucracy" the humanist dimension of the struggle is lost and it is no longer possible to speak of liberation. Hence, our insistence that the authentic solution of the oppressor-oppressed contradiction does not lie in a mere reversal of position in moving from one pole to the other. Nor does it lie in the replacement of the former oppressors with new ones, who continue to subjugate the oppressed- all in the name of their liberation.[8]

While the investigator is aware of the limitations of the study from the point of view of the area covered and the tools adopted for the collection of data, nevertheless, it is felt that the present study helps the social scientist to understand the nature and degree of contradictions that exist in relation to "changing oppressed-oppressor phenomenon" in rural set up.

A further probe involving more sophisticated tools and methods may be necessary for understanding the attitudes of rural leaders with reference to their deep psychological framework towards democratic commitment.

SECTION II

EXPOSURE TO MASS MEDIA, EXTENSION AGENCY CONTACT AND DEMOCRATIC VS. AUTHORITARIAN ATTITUDE

In the foregoing pages the relationship between socio-economic status and democratic vs. authoritarian attitude as found in this study was presented and discussed. What follows hereafter is a discussion of the association between exposure to mass media, extension agency contact, and democratic vs. authoritarian attitude.

It is the concern of all welfare states to bring about a change of outlook among its masses through education and other channels of communication like mass media, community development programmes and extension service. The mass-media and extension agency are considered to be important variables in the process of modernisation, and represent the major forces of social change.[9]

In a discussion guide prepared for the participants by the UNESCO Secretariat it is suggested that "Societies, whatever the degree of their evolution and their political, economic and social structures, cannot achieve optimum development and renew their resources without active, conscious and freely given participation by the population as a whole—participation by the citizens which is itself determined by their abilities, knowledge, attitudes, and behaviour, created or strengthened by education, which provides both knowledge and capacity for clear critical reasoning of the context, nature, and forms of information, disseminated by mass media."[10]

Mass media plays an effective role by conveying identical messages to large number of persons, who are often physically separated, through its varied forms like, newspapers, books, films, filmstrips, motion pictures *etc.*[11] The role of mass media and its penetrating influence on the behaviour of the people is widely recognised. It has been the experience of many developing countries that modern mass-media techniques have greater liberating power than formal education. The popularity of educational mass-media may lead to compete with, even to eliminate some forms of schools.[12] Mass media has greater effects on the society. It appears to achieve the objectives of the state which could not achieve them in spite of its efforts to spread formal education.

In the earlier context school was considered to be the only source of education, the only agent in bringing awareness and the only source of promoting knowledge among people. This claim of formal education is disproved by the advent of technological advancement, particularly the ever growing techniques of mass-media. Now the school is one of the sources of knowledge and information available to those privileged few who can reach it. An individual with a schooled mind conceives of the world as a pyramid of classified packages accessible only to those who carry proper tags.[13] The claim of the school that it is the only source of knowledge should disappear and equal emphasis must be placed on other sources of learning like mass-media, education *etc.* The mass media are considered to be the most powerful media as they do have the power to change attitudes, conduct and behaviour, Nelson B. Henry[14] writing on the social impact of the mass media observes: "certainly whatever potentialities the content of a communication possesses for the modification of human attitudes and opinion, or for the changing of human action, these become enormously magnified when a single communication reaches a vast audience. The political and social symbol of a society, the images of its leaders, its angels and its demons, and the patterns of its mythology may be transmitted to millions of persons simultaneously, not neutrally and impartially as we like to assert, but always in a directed context. The television equipment transmits the sound and visual images of a political figure delivering a speech and, while the sound of the speaker`s voice is still being transmitted, the camera focusses on a sleeping member of the audience or on the rows of empty seats at the back of the auditorium."

As Hocking[15] observes, the importance and prevalence of the mass-media in any society imposes on them an obligation of social responsibility. This is more true in societies wedded to democratic philosophy. A democratic government rests on the assumption that the people are capable of governing themselves better than any one or a few can do it for them. If the citizens are to rule themselves wisely, they must be aware of the issues and problems at stake and must have access to views and information on which to base sound decisions.[16] Therefore, the mass-media must serve as an engine of democracy, as a transmission belt between the people and their elected representatives. Every political system or for that matter any system, maintains a communication net work. The advent of science and technology has revolutionised this network. It is only through the flow of information and exchange of ideas which form the content of a communication system that political relationships can be activised, sustained and put to some use.[17] The very success of government may depend in large measure on the extent to which the press services the political system and the extent to which the people make wise use of the press.[18]

Mass communication media today enable the goverment machineries to penetrate deep into the socio-cultural environments of people which was not possible through earlier forms of communications techniques.Though mass media are viewed apparently as sources of recreation for the common masses, in reality they are objective based and directed towards personal liberation and development of man from his traditional, psychological and mental slavery.

It is difficult to assess the far reaching influence of mass media particularly on those who have been culturally deprived. An attempt is made in this investigation to examine the relation between the vital influence of mass media and democratic outlook of the respondents, measured in terms of their predisposition to changing social situations in the context of our transition — a movement from "tradition to modernity, and from authoritarian social order to democratic living".

By applying the fact that the modern mass media aims at promoting the democratic values, it has been assumed that a great degree of democratic behaviour has been produced with a higher degree of exposure of rural leaders to mass media and extension agency contact.

In some of the studies undertaken on mass media and community leadership, the authors conceded that the degree of exposure to mass media and extension agency contacts form an important variable in studying the progressive leadership in communities. Abraham,[19] Pradipto Roy,[20] Fliegal[21] and others ascribed very high predictive validity to mass media variables and reported significant relatio between mass-media, extension agency contact, interaction with urbanites and village level leadership. Study undertaken by Lalit K. Sen[22] indicates that leaders as compared to non-leaders have high level of contact with extension agency and high degree of exposure to mass media.

It may be noted, however, that these studies were undertaken more than a decade back and much had been accomplished both in mass media techniques and the objective based programmes of mass media, though much still remains to be done.

In view of this it is felt necessary to involve the mass media dimension as one of the variables in the study and examine its impact on the pattern of leadership and the leaders' outlook towards democratic vs. authoritarian attitude.

For the purpose of the study a scale with 15 items was developed to measure the degree of extension agency contact and media exposure, and was administered to 502 respondents. The following is the frequency distribution of extension agency contact and media exposure scores of the respondents.

Class Interval	Frequency
9 - 14	28
15 - 20	121
21 - 26	117
27 - 32	146
33 - 38	71
39 - 44	19
Total	502

Mean 25.49 Standard Deviation: 7.48

The distribution of leaders on extension agency contact and media exposure scale indicates that majority of the leaders have greater contacts with extension agency and exposure of mass media (Mean score: 25.49).

The study examined the relation between media exposure, extension agency contact and the democratic vs. authoritarian attitude by formulating the following hypothesis:

Greater the degree of extension agency contact and media exposure, higher is the degree of democratic attitude.

The coefficients of correlation between extension agency contact, media exposure and democratic attitude of the respondents was computed by using the product moment method. The following table shows the coefficients of correlation between media exposure, extension agency contact and democratic vs. auhoritarian attitude for different samples.

Considering the total population, as can be observed from the above table, there is a high degree of positive correlation between the degree of exposure to mass-media, extension agency contacts and the democratic vs. authoritarian behaviour of rural leaders (r. 0.69 significant at 0.01 level).

The results indicate that in the case of formal leaders, there is more pronounced relationship between media-exposure, extension agency contact, and democratic attitude, where in the case of informal leaders though there is an indication of positive significant relationship between mass-media exposure, extension agency contact and democratic attitude, it is low when compared to formal leaders.

TABLE 6.2

Table showing the coefficients of correlation between the levels of exposure to mass media, extension agency contact and democratic vs. authoritarian attitude for the total group and the sub-groups within the total group

Sample	*Number*	*Coefficient of Correlation*	*'t' value*	*Levels of significance*
Total Group	502	0.69	21.28	0.01
Formal Leaders	288	0.65	19.31	0.01
Informal Leaders	214	0.27	4.28	0.01

Discusion of the Findings

The positive relation noted between the two variables, *i.e.* the mass media exposure and extension agency contact and the democratic vs. authoritarian behaviour of leaders, needs no special interpretation. It has been the philosophy and policy of all governments to use mass-media as an instrument to propagate the democratic ideology in their respective countries. In view of the penetrating influence of a powerful objective based communication system like mass- media it is no suprise that the people who have been exposed to its influence are oriented towards the democratic outlook of life.

The above findings, indicating a positive relationship between the two variables, support empirically the logical relationship conceived in the present investigation.

As mass media is one of the important alternative channels of education in addition to formal systems of education and serves as a powerful instrument in promoting democratic methods of living, it is necessary to evaluate its influence continuously to restructure its programmes according to the changing needs of the community.

In this context the issues like access to media, and the need for the levels of decentralization of media, designing programmes in terms of the needed rural awareness, the objectives of education to which greater considerations should be given, the need for producers and users to consult each other when programmes are being prepared, and the question of setting up structures for systematic co-operation between those responsible for rural education programmes and those responsible for the nation, may be considered as crucial.

In this context mass media planners should be supplied from time to time with feed-back, based on empirical researches for continuous restructuring of its functions. Obviously this involves an assessment of the changing rural situation with special reference to the role of mass media and its impact and providing and laying a foundation for building an edifice for the mass media bearing a direct relationship between the mass media and the social change.

By involving new sophisticated research designs, it may be possible to find out not only the degree of influence of mass media on the democratic outlook of the rural leaders but also the qualitative differences in their outlook with reference to their behavioural dimension.

SECTION III

LEVELS OF ASPIRATIONS AND DEMOCRATIC VS. AUTHORITARIAN ATTITUDE

In the foregoing pages the influence of mass media and extension agency on the democratic vs. authoritarian attitudes of the rural leaders, as found in this study, was discussed. In this section discussion of the relationship between aspiration levels and the democratic attitudes of the rural leaders is presented.

One of the most outstanding social manifestations of the theme of pluralistic life in India has been "hierarchy".[23] Indian society, therefore, has fixed the psychology of various social groups and has evolved minutely graded levels of social distance, and superior inferior relationships, resulting in a hierarchical-pyramidical social structure with a mass of untouchables at its base and a small stratum of elite, the Brahmins, almost equally unapproachable at its apex.[24] The tolerance of differences and the value of harmony could help and sustain the continuity of the social order for centuries in this country.

The belief in teleological order of the universe, the doctrine of *Karma* and transcendentalism further reinforced the belief in social differences and social hierarchy.[25] People occupying different positions in the social ladder starting from the bottom cross section of the pyramid to the apex were guided and regulated by a notion that their life and social status was divinely ordained and therefore unalterable.

It is only after independence, significant programmes have been undertaken to change this age-old belief system and transform their life and status in terms of free social mobility.

In this endeavour India, like any other developing country, believes in raising the levels of aspirations among the masses through the process of modernization. Aspirations to see the major world, to compete for social mobility, and to protect their constitutional guarantees which were the result of a social transition in the country.

A methodological comparison of the traditional-rural community with modernizing society, highlighting a few salient differences, would reveal the landscape through which young leaders are making their way. It is possible that the rural masses in general and leaders in particular witness a change from an inegalitarian hierarchical society to an egalitarian society, from a society in which the basic needs are often the only needs to be satisfied to a society in which the secondary and anticipatary needs are also promised to be satisfied.

Therefore, the revolution of rising levels of aspirations in India to which many contemporary social scientists refer appears to be a phenomenon, resulting from ever increasing aspirations to aspire, to move towards a goal, to live a meaningful life.[26]

In such a context, it is relevant to examine the aspirations of the rural leaders by raising question like whether such aspirations for social mobility characterise all leaders drawn from different social groups—irrespective of their personal, social background and living conditions. It is also the concern of the present study to examine the relationship of these aspirations of the rural leaders with their democratic vs. authoritarian behaviour.

It is presumed in this study that the leaders with higher levels of aspirations are better inclined towards democratic processes in the community than those who hold low levels of aspirations.

This premise emanates from the logic that India has been a closed society, where people believed in authoritarian social order organised in terms of caste dominance, submissiveness, superordinate and subordinate relationships. Those who hold such values tend to be conformists and, therefore, accept their position as unalterable in the system.

The rising aspirations are essentially a phenomenon generating from modern social values where people exercise their democratic rights and aims for social mobility. The desire to be and to live one's own life in terms of the set goals itself reflects their positive outlook for democratic order of life and, therefore, the rising aspirations of a person should be viewed as an essential characteristic of democratic attitude.

This dialectical relationship between the levels of aspirations and democratic attitude, therefore, led to the formulation of the following hypothesis:

> *Higher the levels of aspiration, greater would be the democratic attitude of the leaders.*

As discussed in Chapter 3, the levels of aspirations among the respondents were identified by asking close-ended questions regarding their expectations about education, income and leadership position.

The scores of these sub-areas put together were considered the aspiration level.

The following is the frequency distribution of 502 respondents on aspiration levels.

Class Interval	*Frequency*
10-12	29
13-15	138
16-18	85
19-21	131
22-24	84
25-27	25
28-30	10
Total	502

Mean: 18.296 Standard Deviation: 2.84

Correlational Analysis

To test the relationship between aspiration levels and democratic attitude, Pearson's 'r' was computed, which gives the degree and direction of relationship. The following table presents the coefficients of correlation between the levels of aspiration and democratic attitude obtained forthe total population and sub-groups within the population.

TABLE 6.3

Table showing the co-efficients of correlation between the levels of aspiration and democratic vs. authoritarian attitude of total group and sub-groups within the total group

Sample	*Number*	*Co-efficient of Correlation*	*'t' value*	*Level of significance*
Total Sample	502	+ 0.592	16.46	0.01
Formal leaders	288	+ 0.505	15.45	0.01
Informal leaders	214	+ 0.645	16.068	0.01

The above table indicates that there is a positive, significant relationship between the levels of aspirations and democratic behaviour (r.=59, significant at .01 level). The data analysed separately for formal and informal leaders revealed that the relationship between the aspirations and the democratic attitude, for both the samples, is positive and highly significant. High aspiration level of rural leaders typically indicates high democratic attitude and low aspiration level indicates the authoritarian attitude. There is no significant variation in over all relationship on account of formal positions in village Panchayats.

Discussion of the Findings

A positive relationship between the levels of aspirations and the degree of democratic attitude is discovered in this study (r = + 0.59). As discussed earlier, the high aspirations of the leaders may be due to the impact of industrialization and implementation of programmes of planned change. India has taken significant measures for the betterment of village communities and to modernise its masses. The main objectives of these planned programmes of change are to improve the standards of living and to build up high aspirations among the masses for their economic and social progress.

High aspirations of leaders noted in this study may be the resultant of an interaction of education and changing philosophy of people in general. It needs no emphasis that it is only the force and process of democratization that result in high aspirations and vice versa.

While the findings of the present study cannot be compared directly with those of other researches because this problem hardly has been examined in India; some imterpretations of the same can be offered in the light of the vast theoretical material accumulated in this area. For instance Parsons argues: "Supported by a belief in an open class system, individual mobility orientations have been deeply rooted in all democratic societies."[27] Applied to the Indian conditions, it is possible to assume that the Indian leaders would aspire for such mobility and constantly aim at higher goals in tefms of education, occupation and income and all possible avenues of progress.

Therefore, the findings of the present study can be logically explained in terms of the theoretical framework offered by Parsons.

The reasons for the rising aspirations in the present context in India can be linked with industrialization and implementation of programmes of planned change, it may be noted that India, like any other industrializing society, believes in emphasising and encouraging high aspirations for its success. This has been spelt out in the objectives of community development. In all `open' societies, such goals are firmly internalized, even while they realise that the world is not entirely at their disposal.

Without making any value judgement of the desirability of such change we may have to accept that Indian society is committed to modernization not only in terms of its material and technological basis but also in terms of its associated social structure. It needs no emphasis that only the forces and process of democratization lead to high aspirations among people. Therefore, the positive association between the democratic vs. authoritarian behaviour and the levels of aspirations of rural leaders is in congruence with the theoretical rationale.

It is interesting to note that in the modern context of our traditional philosophy, belief system is undergoing rapid transformation as evinced in this study. The achievement motivation and aspirations for success in life are essentially attributed to modernization.[28] The leaders appear to have internalised the new values like belief in progress and achievement which is reflected in their aspirations. The high aspirations on the part of the leaders is indicative of the fact that the spiritual values of Indian community are being replaced by material and economic values. High aspirations of leaders noted in this study may be an outcome of the influence of education, and changing philosophy of people.

SECTION IV

SOCIAL AWARENESS AND DEMOCRATIC VS. AUTHORITARIAN ATTITUDE

In the foregoing pages the findings of relationship between levels of aspirations and degree of democratic attitude were presented and discussed. In the following pages the association between social awareness and democratic vs. authoritarian attitude of rural leaders, as found in the present study, will be discussed.

In most of the underdeveloped nations and more so in India, large sectors of populations have been segregated from the mainstream of life for many centuries. People in India suffered suppression due to built-in socio-cultural mechanism of discrimination and certain dominant ethos of life built around inequality, the doctrine of 'Karma' and so on.[29] The social, cultural and historical forces have contributed to many social evils resulting in a scoial order which was synonymous with the "Culture of Silence",[30] as explained by Paulo Freire.

As India is committed to social equality and a true democratic life, much has been said on the need for the social awareness and the role of education as a cultural action[31] to emancipate people from the traditional evils of life. Emergence of such social awareness to which Paulo Freire refers to as 'conscientization' implies not only awareness among people of their socio-cultural reality but also the implications of such awareness and consequences of their action upon this reality to transform.[32] The social awareness, therefore, is the absolute need to overcome the culture of silence and to ensure true democratic social order.

After independence, the country has embarked on several programmes to set up a democratic social order and 33 years of experience has taught us the importance of such social awareness among our masses, not only for humanistic values but also for the smooth functioning of the system. But paradoxically many people in India, even today, appear to be not aware of what their rights are, and the duties that go with these rights. Therefore it is necessary to reflect upon the course of conscientization in this country measured in terms of the rising levels of social awareness among the people through empirical investigations, and the present study is an attempt in this direction.

It has been the objective of the present study to limit its scope to a few selected rural leaders who have started undergoing this process after independence. In designing the research, the investigator has made an attempt to measure the levels of social awareness among rural leaders with regard to the existing socio-cultural conditions and the changes occurring in the social, economic and political institutions.

It is relevant at this stage to refer to some of the dominant degenerated social practices in the country which have been responsible for an unjust social order in the culture of silence. The rural credit system, the bonded labour, child marriages, male ascendancy, the traditional concept of chastity, marital status of women have played a decisive role in the material and cultural life of the people in the community influencing the psychological make up of the people and their social outlook. The popular masses have started undergoing this process of conscientization especially during the last thirty years of our independence under the influence of the rural development schemes, mass media, the elections and so on.

It is interesting to note that these masses appear to be going exactly through a phase which Paulo Freire describes as a 'Naive transitivity' [33] which is a state in which people are able to distinguish clearly the fact that they are being exploited and are able to transcend their concrete socio-cultural reality.[33a] In this phase of 'Naive transitivity' people however may not be really sure of what they want to do or what they can do with their new-found consciousness, with the result they may either allow to continue the earlier order of the society, with a compromise or take up a righteous stand with indignant behaviour. The recent class war in Indian context appears to be an outcome of this situation.[34]

This situation is an explosive one and needs a careful handling and treatment from the leaders of the people at all levels. Therefore, an investigation into the awareness of the leaders and their commitment to the changing social institutions has been considered imperative from the point of view of the present study. The role requirement of leadership under the new circumstances has to be specific and geared to achievement rather than diffused and status quo oriented.

Social awareness in this context has been conceived as problem consciousness implying a desire on the part of the leaders to overthrow the traditional injustices and create a new social order.

Social awareness therefore is defined, in this study, as a knowledge of the social, economic and political change and new institutions and the inclination towards achieving these changes (change of outlook). So social awareness is characterised by the following dimensions.

(a) a knowledge of the existence of the new institutions and changes;

(b) attitude towards the desirability of these changes and new institutions;

(c) feeling regarding the possibility of attaining these changes.

These three levels of information put together will be known as the "social awareness of the individual".

As social awareness is conceived an essential and integral component of democratic living, it implies that a man with higher levels of social awareness will be psychologically pre-disposed to a democratic social order.

In order to test this relationship between the levels of social awareness and the democratic outlook of the leaders, emerging out of the above *a priori*, the following hypothesis has been formulated and tested.

Higher the level of social awareness of the leaders, greater is their democratic attitude.

To find out the relationship between social awareness and democratic attitude a scale was prepared on the basis of the above definition involving the programmes of changes like new educational opportunities, new credit facilities, medical facilities, owner-tenant relationships, abolition of child labour and child marriages, abolition of dowry, *etc.* Centring around these themes, question items were prepared and the scale was administered to 502 respondents.

The frequency distribution of the scores on social awareness of 502 respondents is given below:

Range	Frequency
80-89	4
90-99	21
100-109	44
110-119	73
120-129	141
130-139	154
140-149	57
150-159	8
Total	502

Range: 80 -159

Mean: 125,62 Standard Deviation: 14.03

The study has revealed that there is considerable level of social awareness on the part of leaders (125.62= mean). The new leaders in the rural set up today are receptive to the changes and they look at the changes not only as desirable but also possible. These findings are in conformity with findings of an earlier study[35], where the leaders are found to be conscious about political and social problems. The findings of the present study are very crucial to all those who are concerned with the rural programmes. It has been the popular opinion that the masses in the villages are ignorant and suffer from want of proper guidance. For instance in a study undertaken by Mishra [36] it is revealed that leaders are not well aware of the current problems and changes due to illiteracy and lack of media exposure. The present study, as against the above mentioned, revealed greater awareness among the rural leaders. The study clearly established the changing levels of social awareness among leaders, which is a matter of high gratification to social scientists and community level workers. They have considerable insights about the planned programmes and modern institutions and they are no more guided by traditional methods and beliefs. It is interesting to note that they not only consider changes desirable but also possible.

Correlational Analysis

The coefficient of correlation was worked out for the total population and sub-groups within the population. The table below shows the 't' values obtained between social awareness and democratic attitude of different groups of respondents alongwith the level of significance.

TABLE 6.4

Table showing the coefficients of correlation of social awareness and democratic vs. authoritarian attitude, for total sample and sub-groups within the sample.

Sample	*Number*	*Coefficient of Correlation*	*'t' value'*	*Level of significance*
Total Sample	502	0.81	30.35	0.01
Formal Leader	288	0.72	25.41	0.01
Informal Leader	214	0.83	38.05	0.01

The above data indicate a high degree of positive relationship between the level of social awareness and the democratic vs. authoritarian attitude.

As indicated in the table, an attempt is also made here to analyse the data separately for formal and informal leaders to find out the relationship between the social awarenesss and democratic vs. authoritarian attitude in each case. The findings have indicated a positive relationship between the variables involved in each group.

The results of this study concerning the relationship between social awareness and democratic behaviour now be stated in a summary fashion. The data demonstrates a positive relationship between levels of social awareness and democratic attitude clearly supporting the hypothesis that the respondents identified with higher level of social awareness would tend to exhibit a greater degree of democratic attitude; and those identified with lower level of social awareness would express a lower degree of democratic attitude. The association between the varibles was maintained rather consistently.

As there have been no earlier studies on social awareness related to the democratic attitudes, the findings of the present study stand conspicuous opening up new avenues for further researches.

The findings of the present study in terms of the positive relationship between social awareness and democratic attitude can be understood in the following manner.

Discussion of the Findings

The present study has revealed that the leaders in the rural set-up are receptive to the changes in different institutions and perceive these changes not only as desirable but also as possible.

The present study interestingly supports the popular view that there is a growing awareness among the masses in general and in rural activists in particular.[37] This growing awareness among the rural leaders noted in this study may not however preclude the possibility of carrying with them certain characteristics of the past culture what Freire refers to as 'myths of culture of silence'[38], especially in the Indian context where such leaders have been projected suddenly into a limelight and role enactment situation without sufficient direction.

Therefore, though the present study has indicated in positive terms, the rising levels of awareness among rural leaders, one may have to exercise caution in accepting this fact as being axiomatic. This is so because we cannot totally depend upon the reliability of the present study designed with a limited purpose to identify the levels of awareness. However, it is gratifying to note that the leaders in rural areas are fully conscious of the changes in their environment and they appear to be favourably disposed towards the desirability of the changes. As there are no parallel studies in this area, the findings of the present study cannot be interpreted with a comparative perspective. However, the positive relationship between the levels of social awareness and the attitude towards democratization supports *a priori* and needs no further interpretation. Social awareness is an essential component of democratic life and these variables are complementary to each other. The trend revealed through this study, thus, ensures a sound foundation for the democratic order of life in this country.

Notes and References

1. Charles P. Loomis, "Change in Rural India as Related to Social Power and Sex", *Behavioural Sciences and Community Development,* (Hyderabad, N.I.C.D. Vol. I No.1, March-1967), p. 4.
2. David C. McClelland (1961). *The Achieving Society,* (New York: D. Van Nostrand, Com. Inc.).
3. (i) Mishra, S.N., "Emerging Rural Leadership in Rural India—A case study", *Quarterly Journal of Local Self-Government Institute,* Vol. XVII, No.2, (Oct-Dec. 1976), pp. 189-208.
   (ii) Rajendra Joshi, "Panchayati Raj and Emerging Rural Leadership", *Quarterly Journal of Local Self-Government Institute,* pp. 550-64.
4. Bhatt, K. S., "Emerging Pattern of Leadership in Panchayati Raj set up in Mysore State". In Jacob, George (ed.), *Readings on Panchayat Raj* (Hyderabad, N.I.C.D., 1971), pp. 121-44.
5. (i) *Ibid.*
   (ii) Abida Samiuddin, "The Emerging Pattern of Rural Leadership", *Kurukshetra,* (February, 1977), pp 4-5.
   (iii) Karipurath, Paul, "The Emerging Pattern of Leadership in Mysore State", Administrative Training Institute, Mysore.
6. Baijnath Singh, "The Impact of Community Development Programme on Rural Leadership." In Park and Tinker Irene (ed.), *Leadership and Political Institutions in India. op.cit.,* pp. 358-71.
7. Paulo Freire (1975). *Pedagogy of the Oppressed* (England, Penguin Education, Penguin Books Ltd.).
8. *Ibid,* p. 33.
9. Mathur, J.C. and Paul Neurath, *"An Indian Experiment in Farm Radio Forums",* (UNESCO.1955), p. 105.
10. Robert de Mont Valon, "The Aspirations of Young Migrant Workers in Western Europe," *Educational Studies and Documents,* UNESCO, No.21, 1976.
11. Edgar Dale, (ed.). *Mass Media and Education, The Fifty-third year Book of the National Society for the Study of Education,* (Illinois: NSSE, 1954), p.1.
12. Peter, H. Rossi, Bruce, J. Biddle, (ed), "Educational Media, Education, and Society". In Peter H. Rossi, Bruce, J. Biddle (ed.), *The New Media and Education—Their Impact on Society,* (New York: Anchor Books Doubleday and Company, INC, 1966), p. 47.
13. Ivan Illich. *De-Schooling Society,* (New York: 635, Madison Avenue, Penguin Books, 1977), p. 78.
14. Franklin Fearing, "Social Impact of the Mass Media of Communication". In *Mass Media and Education—The Fifty-third Year Book of the National Society For the Study of Education,* (ed.) by Nelson, B. Henry, (Illinois: NSSE, 1954), pp. 166-67.

15. William E. Hocking, (1947). *Freedom of the Press: A Framework of Principle,* (Chicago. University of Chicago Press.).
16. Theodore Peterson. "The Social Functions of the Press". In *Mass Media And Education—The Fifty-third Year Book of the National Society For the Study of Education,* (ed.), Nelson B. Henry, *op.cit.,* p.33.
17. (i) Lasswell, Harold D. "The Structure and Function of Communication in Society". In Bryson, Lyman (ed.), *The Communication of Ideas,* (New York: Harper and Row, 1948), p. 37.
    (ii) Lasswell, Harold *et. al.* (ed.). *Language of Politics: Studies in Quantitative Semantics,* (The M.I.T. Press,1965).
18. Theodore Peterson: "The Social Functions of the Press", *op.cit.,* p. 33.
19. Francis M. Abraham. *Dynamics of Leadership in Village India,* (Allahabad: India International Publication, 1974), p. 6.
20. Pradipto Roy, "Characteristics of Emerging Leaders". In Vidyarthi L.P. (ed.), *Leadership in India,* (Bombay : Asia Publishing House, 1967).
21. (i) Fliegal, Fredrick, C. and others, *Agricultural Innovations in Indian Villages* , (Hyderabad : N.I.C.D., 1968).
    (ii) Other studies highlighting the use of various media of communication and effectivity in response pattern are: Varma, S.P., Narain, Iqbal and Associates, *Voting Behaviour in a Changing Society* (Delhi. National, 1973) pp. 200-73.
    (iii) Atal, Yogesh. *Local Communities and National Politics,* Part-III (Delhi: National, 1971), pp.135-279.
    (iv) Sirsikar, V.M.. *Sovereigns Without Crown* (Bombay. Popular Prakashan, 1973).
22. Lalit K. Sen. *Opinion Leadership in India* (Hyderabad: N.I.C.D., 1969), p. 56.
23. Thirtha, N.V., *op.cit.*
24. Desai A.R., (1978). *Rural Sociology in India,* (Bombay, Popular Prakashan,), p.54.
25. Thirtha, N.V.,. *A Study in Values, op.cit.*
26. Myrdal Gunnar, (1971) "A Loaded Misconception". In *The Challenge of World Poverty- A World Anti -Poverty Programme in Outline,* (Pelican Books.), p. 375.
27. Talcot Parsons and Edward A. Shills, *Toward A General Theory of Action,* (Cambridge, Harvard University Press, 1952), pp. 80-81.
28. David C. McClelland. *The Achieving Society, op.cit.*
29. Thirtha, N.V., *op.cit.*
30. (i) Paulo Freire, (1977). *Cultural Action for Freedom,* (England: Penguin Books, Ltd). p.16.
    (ii) Paulo Freire, "Cultural Freedom in Latin America". In *Human Rights and the Liberation of Man in the America* (ed), Louis M. Colonese, (Indiana. University of Notre Dame Press, 1970).
31. Paulo Freire, *Cultural Action For Freedom, op.cit.*
32. *Ibid.*
33. *Ibid.*
    (a) The *Karma Phal* theory is no longer accepted and thus one's social status is not seen as the result of one's Karma in a previous life. There is realization among people to certain extent that inequalities are man made. This trend can well be generalized for the whole of India. For details see Frankel, Francine, R, *India's Green Revolution,* (Princeton: University Press, 1971), p. 262.
34. Some of these implications have been discussed by Rajni Kothari in his Introduction to *Caste in Indian Politics,* (Longman: 1970). Also see Andre

Beteille, *Caste Old and New : Essays in Social Structure and Social Stratification*, (Bombay: Asia Publishing House, 1969).

35. (i) Rajendra Joshi, *Panchayati Raj and Emerging Rural Leadership, op.cit.*
    (ii) Mishra, S. N., *op.cit.*
36. Mishra, S.N., "Emerging Leadership in Rural India—A Case Study", *Quarterly Journal of the Local Self-Government Institute*. Vol.XVII, No.2, (Oct.-Dec.-1976), pp.189-208.
37. Malla Reddy, M., *A Few Selected Socio-Psychological Correlates of Activism, op. cit.*
38. Paulo Freire, *Cultural Action for Freedom, op.cit.*,

7

SUMMARY AND CONCLUSIONS

The present investigation as presented in different chapters of this thesis was an attempt to examine the pattern of relationship between social, educational and psychological background of rural leaders and their democratic vs. authoritarian attitude. The democratic vs. authoritarian attitude of the leaders was studied as a psychological predisposition towards a given socio-cultural situation, rather than an actual participation in a situation.

Authoritarianism and democracy are restricted to certain modes of behaviour of rural leaders in situations that are generally faced by the leaders. In this context the authoritarian leader is viewed as one who exerts unlimited power to influence his followers without taking group's concern, who tries to maintain status quo; who resists change, and who is interested in individual benefit rather than the group benefit. Democratic leader on the contrary is viewed as one who exerts limited leadership, who believes in social, economic and political equality, who has positive outlook towards new institutions and planned economic and political changes, and who is interested in working for group benefits.

The present study thus endeavoured to examine closely the pattern of emerging leadership in rural India identified in terms of their socio-economic status, mass media exposure, levels of aspirations and degree of social awareness and democratic vs. authoritarian attitude.

The variables included in the present investigation are (i) socio-economic status,(ii) exposure to mass media and contacts with extension agencies, (iii) levels of aspirations, (iv) democratic vs. authoritarian attitude.

Operational Definitions

Under socio-economic status seven components *.viz.* caste status, education, occupation, income, land holdings, type of house and social participation of the leaders were included. Radio listening, newspaper reading, exposure to movie were taken as exposure to mass media, and contacts with extension officers, village level workers were taken as extension agency contacts. Regarding aspiration levels the study conceived "aspiration as the goal or level of attainment that an individual likes to reach for his success in life". Another important variable of this study, `social awareness` is conceived as "problem consciousness", coupled with a desire on the part of leaders to overthrow traditional injustices and create a new social order. Social awareness is characterised by:

(1) Knowledge about recent socio-economic change and creation of new institutions.

(2) Attitude towards "the desirability of these changes and new institutions".

(3) Confidence regarding the possibility of attaining these changes. Thus social awareness is conceived in terms of these three dimensional behaviour of the leaders.

The following hypotheses were formulated within a rationale built up through relevant discussions.

1. *Higher the level of socio-economic status of the respondents, greater would be the degree of their democratic attitude.*

2. *Greater the degree of extension agency contact the media exposure of the respondents, higher would be the degree of their democratic attitude.*

3. *Higher the levels of aspirations of the respondents, greater would be the degree of democratic attitude.*

4. *Higher the levels of social awareness of the respondents, greater would be the degree of their democratic attitude.*

Research Procedures

The present investigation was designed as quantitative empirical field study. In view of this, certain tools had to be constructed, which are as follows:

Name of the Tool	*Varibale Measures*
Democratic vs. authoritarian attitude scale	Democratic vs. authoritarian behaviour.
Socio-economic status scale	Socio-economic status.
Aspiration scale	Levels of Aspiration.
Mass Media exposure scale	Levels of exposure to mass media and contacts with extension agencies.
Social awareness scale.	Social awareness.

Keeping the design of the study and the past researches in view, the specific tools were selected.

The Preliminary Study

A preliminary study was conducted to pre-test the tools from the point of view of determining their suitability and establishing their validity and reliability. Accepted statistical procedures were adopted to carry out an items analysis.

Subjects

The subjects selected for the investigation are 502 rural leaders drawn from thirty villages of five districts in Telangana region. Both formal leaders and informal leaders are included in the sample. Members elected to the village Panchayats including the Panchayat presidents were taken as formal leaders, whereas the informal leaders were identified by adopting reputational method. Thus 288 formal leaders and 214 informal leaders were included in the study. The sample was selected through multistage purposive sampling technique.

Having presented the details regarding the objectives, variables, hypotheses, sample and the tools employed, an attempt is made here to present the significant findings of the investigation. Following this, some of the limitations of the present investigation, the implication of the findings of the study for curricular programmes and suggestion for future researches are also presented.

Socio-Economic Status and Democratic vs. Authoritarian Attitude

A general observation of leadership pattern in traditional Indian rural community suggests that the leadership pattern was associated with privileged caste groups, context bound, defined by socio-cultural conditions, and built around ascriptive method of transfer of power. Thus the sources of recruitment of leaders were closed and predetermined.

After Independence, in view of the nation's commitment to principles of equality and democracy, several steps have been taken to bring about necessary transformation among its people. Institutions like universal adult franchise, civil rights, equality before law, well developed education system *etc.* appear to have influenced the leadership structure in the country.

The present study has revealed that there is considerable transformation with regard to the leadership pattern in rural India. A change in the recruitment pattern is evinced in the present investigation. It is interesting to note that majority of the respondents falls in the middle socio-economic background and evidently there is considerable representation of leaders from the lower sections of population also.

The findings of this investigation have supported the hypothesis formulated, by revealing a positive relationship between the socio-economic status and democratic attitude of the leaders.

It is significant to note from the findings of this study that today's leaders are not only recruited from all groups and segments of rural community, but also have a positive orientation towards democratic processes which indeed is a very important transformation.

Exposure to Mass Media and Extension Agency contacts and Democratic vs. Authoritarian Behaviour

The second variable selected for this investigation was the degree of exposure to mass media and extension agency contacts of the rural leaders. The findings have confirmed the hypothesis by revealing a positive relationship between media exposure, extension agency contacts and democratic attitude (r=.69 significant at 0.01 level).

Media exposure and extension agency contacts were considered by many investigators variables, which influence the outlook of the individuals. Most of the developing countries are making efforts to bring change in outlook among their masses through education, mass media, extension services *etc*. Many investigators have studied these variables in relation to their leadership pattern.

The findings of the present study, are in congruence with the study done by Saran, where he observed that one's media habit and contacts are related to the larger process of modernization.

It is no surprise that the people who have been exposed to mass media's influence are oriented towards the democratic outlook of life as the influence of mass media creates consciousness among leaders to prefer politeness, adopt methods of appeal and persuasions, and seek the support of all sections of the commmunity for the stability and popularity of their leadership.

Levels of Aspiration and Democratic Behaviour of the Rural Leaders

The, third variable selected for this investigation was the levels of aspirations, of rural leaders in relation to their democratic vs. authoritarian attitude. The findings once again have confirmed the hypothesis that there is a positive relationship between aspiration levels of leaders and their democratic attitude (r . 59 significant at 0.01 levels).

The rising levels of aspiration in the present context in India can be linked with Industrialization. India as any other industrialising society believes in emphasizing and encouraging high aspirations for success. One of the objectives of community development was to raise the expectations of the masses, which was considered necessary under the assumption that increased expectations would lead to putting in increased productive efforts. The social, cultural, political and economic changes introduced in the society infused newer values among the people, which has resulted in increasing aspirations towards social mobility. The achievement motivation and aspirations for success in life are essentially the attributes of modernisation. The leaders appear to have internalised the new values like belief in progress and achievement which must have reflected in their aspirations.

Social Awareness and Democratic vs. Authoritarian Attitude

The fourth variable in this investigation was the social awareness of the leaders. It was hypothesised that there would be a positive relationship between the degree of social awareness and the democraitc attitude. Our findings to a significant degree, supported the hypothesis formulated (r= .81 significant at .01 level).

For centuries larger sections of population have been suppressed and segregated from the mainstream of life. Several social, cultural and historical forces have contributed to many social evils resulting in a social order with a syndrome of "culture of silence".

India is now committed to social equality and the democratic system of governance. In this connection several efforts are being made, and many programmes are introduced, to create a democratic social order, and to bring about scoial awareness among masses. On the basis of the findings of this study, one may draw an inference that, these programmes have created a great degree of impact on the leaders and has sown seeds of social awakening and problem consciousness among masses. Social awareness is an essential component of democratic life which evidently has influenced their behaviour towards democratic process.

Discussion of the Findings and the Policy Implications

India with more than 700 million population with a cultural history stretching back to 3000 years is passing today through a cultural transition characterised by number of significant changes in social, economic and political life of the people. This social transformation is because of a planned change and also as a result of certain natural forces. In pursuance of our planned social change, many forces and factors have been at work such as means of transportation and communications, industrialisation, secular education system, universal adult franchise, the introduction of democratic decentralization, and emphasis on community development. The social scientist analyst is very often struck up by a series of paradoxes while evaluating the nature of changes that have taken place in Indian society.

What is interesting to a social scientist is democratic planning as visualised in India presents specific difficulties,not in common with developing countries. Democratic processes here are complex as the conflicting pulls of traditional ideology are apt to generate friction and slow down the place of change.

One of the important reasons for such paradoxes is the communication system built between policy makers and the rural masses through different intermediate agencies. Rural leaders form a strong link between the policy makers and governmental machinery on the one hand, and the rural masses on the other, and many of our policies and programmes are translated into action only through this segment of rural community.

It has been often felt that many policies framed at the top are not implemented either due to the communication gap that exists between the policy makers and the executors of the policy or due to distorted communication generating "noise" in the communication channel. Unless the rural leaders who form a link between policy makers and rural masses, are psychologically predisposed in favour of these policies and commit themselves to implement such policies, it is difficult to shape the destiny of the nation.

Therefore, it was considered crucial in this study to examine socio-psychological background of rural leaders with special reference to their democratic attitude. The findings of the present study which focused on socio-cultural background of rural leaders, their levels of aspirations, degree of awareness and attitude towards the process of democratization may be viewed as significant contribution to educational workers, social scientists and governmental machinery, dealing with the rural developmental programmes.

The study has revealed very important developments in rural life in general and rural leadership pattern in particular. As already stated the study has revealed that the leaders today unlike in the past come from all levels of social strata and leadership is no more the privilege of the higher echelons of the society. The study also indicated that leaders maintain a close rapport with government machinery and extension officials and are deeply influenced by the mass media programmes and extension agency contacts. They have exhibited a high degree of aspirations and of social awareness and have also expressed a positive orientation towards democratic process taking place in the country.

Thus the recent flux in education, improved mass-media, increasing community activities appear to have produced such pervasive influences on the leaders as it would be extremely difficult to trace its deep rooted ramifications.

> In Parsons'[1] terminology, developed countries are characterized by the prevalence of achievement norms, universalism and specificity, whereas underdeveloped countries are characterized by ascriptive norms, particularism and diffuseness. That is, in developed countries people are evaluated in terms of what they can do (achieved status) rather than in terms of what they are (ascribed status) anyone is at least ideallly able to compete for any job (universalism), rather than being permitted only to do particular jobs as in a caste system (particularism) and the raltionship of one man to another is typically more specific, or limited to the labour contract, rather than diffuse as in a traditional society where economic-relationships are tied intimately to all sorts of other relationships involving kinship, political, religious and other social structures.

Some of these attributes which characterize the social, economic and political life of developing countries appear to be undergoing rapid transformation in Indian context. It has been the concern of all societies to raise the aspirations of their masses and India is no exception. The present study has revealed that respondents have high aspirations measured in terms of their vocational, educational and political goals. By implication, such explosion of rising aspirations can lead to either social reconstruction or social destruction, depending on the socio-cultural context in which people live and the means that they adopt to achieve these goals.

According to David C. McClelland[2] the greater achievements are motivated by strong desires on the part of at least some people in the culture and the factor of achievement-motive is partly responsible, for economic growth which is a positive side of this socio-psychological phenomenon. But a pause here to speculate on the casual chain of rising aspirations in a social climate is peculiar, paradoxical and at times paranoid as ours.

To examine the picture from a different angle; India is strictly speaking a "Soft State".[3] The underdeveloped countries are all, albeit in varying degrees, `Soft States'. This stands out as a significant feature among the conditions that together have made it an underdeveloped one.

The term "Soft State" is understood to imply all the various types of social indiscipline which mainfest themselves by: deficiencies in legislation and in particular law observance and enforcement, a widespread disobedience by public officials on various levels to rules and directives handed down to them, and often collusion with powerful persons and groups of persons whose conduct they should regulate. Within the concept of the `Soft State' belongs also corruption. These several patterns of behaviour are interrelated in the sense that they permit or even provoke each other in circular causation having cumulative effects.[4] Further, Myrdal observes "The laxity and arbitrariness in a national community that can be characterized as a soft state can be, and are, "exploited for personal gains by people who have economic, social and political power".[5] While the opportunties for large scale exploitation opened up by the soft state, are only at the disposal of the upper strata, even persons quite low in the social ladder often find opportunities for petty gains.[6]

Under these conditions, rising aspirations in the absence of desirable value orientations may result or probably has already resulted in a number of undesirable consequences. The rising aspirational levels have to be viewed from its general correlation to the 'Soft State' structures and in particular its relationship with the quality of the existing opportunity structure.

Implicit in the concept of 'Soft State' is the existence of an illegitimate opportunity structure, that guarantees success, not on the basis of merit but on back door methods. With rising aspirations, people more often than not tend to patronize such a structure which sponsors an easy way to success. In the absence of aspirations illegitimate opportunity structures will not have an effect of great magnitude, but this structure combined with rising opportunities logically would result in an unhealthy social phenomenon.

Rising opportunities as an isolated factor or under the existing circumstances by no means an unambiguous benefit. Implicit in the promotion of aspirations is the promotion of proper values. Education should develop strong ethical values which not only sees that the individual works under constitutional norms but also opposes the illegitimate opportunity structures. Every type of motivational force should be under the aegis of reasoning and within the framework of institutionalized competition.

Rising level of social awareness is yet another very important finding of the study, the subtle implications of which need to be understood with adequate care.

As stated earlier the peculiarities of the problem of development of underdeveloped countries stem from varied sociological problems apart from economic problems. For centuries, sections of Indian society have been exploited, without any semblance of hope for redemption. The indoctrination of various ideologies at various levels like doctrine of *Karma,* Transcendentalism and Renunciation, has been so intense, that many did not know if any other kind of life existed. The masses existed as beings which are a temporal and which cannot objectify their existence.

However, after the independence the country committed itself to an egalitarian philosophy and consequently, set about to educate the masses of their conditions and that better life existed and was within the realms of their reach. This was the first attempt made to promote social awareness, and judging from the results of this study, it appears to be quite successful.

But then the question is about the kind of social awareness that is envisaged and needs to be promoted. A social awareness that constitutes only problem consciousness without some direction and commitment is certainly not desirable. Awareness and non commitment actions should not lead to dehumanization, but should act as a solution to the problems of ignorance and eradication of social evils.

What is peculiar about the rising social awareness is that it has manifested itself purely in the form of individual awareness. People have come to acknoweldge and accept the rights of the individual *vis-a-vis* themselves, but they have not been taught that rights call for certain mandatory obligations towards the society. So the question then is what type of an awareness? If awareness should be brought about by educating the masses from the view-point of a broader social context, they should be made to understand that exploitation was the effect, a kind of institutionalised life which is undesirable in the modern context for anybody. Both the downtrodden as well as the upper strata should be taught that rights for the individual should be respected, and that these rights carry certain duties to ensure a better future.

Policy makers dealing with both formal and non-formal systems of education should build the learning activities and experiences around such "centres" of curriculum. These activities should not only generate forces which help the people in breaking off from the undesirable past but also in integrating them into a "socialistic democratic society".

However, present investigator is careful in judging the "effects" of such raising aspirations and changing phenomenon of social awareness, as much more sophisticated researches involving "longitudinal designs" need be undertaken before incorporating curricular changes.

In spite of several limitations that are noted in a study like the present one, one may safely conclude that extension agency activities, mass-media programmes if they are more pragmatic can act as powerful weapons to bring about a social reconstruction. Rural leaders with their aspirations and social awareness given the right direction through 'curricular programmes' can help in breaking psychological and emotional ties of the people from unhealthy traditions and convert them into new men and women with new commitments, new work habits and new values of life.

Suggestions for Future Studies

The following are some of the potential areas for undertaking research by educational workers and social scientists.

For the present, it seems logical to concentrate on some of the significant correlations between the leaders' attitude towards democratic processes and their other socio-psychological correlates involving more sophisticated research designs which might further help in providing more appropriate interpretations and conceiving more pragmatic implications. In any case much remains to be done in unravelling the fascinating association between the complex social changes taking place in the country and emerging leadership pattern. The major problem needs to be examined is: the relationship between the socio-psychological correlates of an individual in relation to his leadership role in the society at different levels.

For obvious reasons the present study has been limited to only a small section of rural leaders at the grassroots level. The major concern of social scientists should logically focus on conducting the studies involving leaders at different levels from diverse populations from diverse settings and with use of diverse research designs. In other words studies on the following lines might provide broad guidelines for future research.

1. With regard to the design of the study this was a correlational one. Employment of a longitudinal design might bring out a few more significant results and reveal the real impact of developmental programmes undertaken over a period of time on the rural masses in general and the rural leaders in particular. Such studies should, however, possibly be undertaken by the departments of universities or research bureaus.

2. Covering additional villages from other regions in the state and

employing a number of other variables particularly the political ideology, party affiliation of leaders might provide the investigators in the field in with deeper insights into the problems.

3. Studying the general behavioural characteristics of leaders in comparison to the rest of the population in the community, interactional patterns and communication net-work within different levels and types of leadership, are some of the vital areas which need to be explored by the social scientists in the country.

4. Employment of techniques like projective techniques, depth interview and participant observation methods, might help in understanding the complex behaviour of rural leaders,

Notes and References

1. Talcot Parsons, Quoted in David. C. McClelland, *The Achieving Society,* (New York: D.Van Nostrand Com. Inc. 1961), pp. 16-17.
2. David C. McClelland, *op. cit.* pp 16-17.
3. Myrdal, Gunnar, "The Soft State". In *The Challenge of World Poverty—A World Anti-Poverty Programme in Outline,* (Australia: Penguin Books Ltd. 1970), pp.211-51.
4. *Ibid.*
5. *Ibid.*
6. *Ibid.*

Appendices

Appendix - I

SOCIO-ECONOMIC STATUS SCALE

Village : **District :**

1. Name: ( )
2. Age : ( )
3. Male/Female ( )
4. Caste :
   - (i) Scheduled Caste/Scheduled Tribe ( )
   - (ii) Backward Caste ( )
   - (iii) Forward Caste ( )
5. Educational Background of the respondents :
   - (i) Illiterate ( )
   - (ii) Primary or literate ( )
   - (iii) Middle School ( )
   - (iv) High School ( )
   - (v) Intermediate ( )
   - (vi) Graduation ( )
   - (vii) Professional/Post-Graduation ( )
6. Occupation:
   - (i) Agriculture Labour ( )
   - (ii) Caste Occupation ( )

(iii) Business ( )

(iv) Independent profession ( )

(v) Service ( )

7. Respondents' family income (annual) all sources:

(i) Below Rs.500.00 ( )

(ii) Rs.501-1000 ( )

(iii) Rs.1001-2000 ( )

(iv) Rs.2001-3000 ( )

(v) Rs.3001-4000 ( )

(vi) Rs.4001-5000 ( )

(vii) Rs.5001-6000 ( )

(viii) Rs.6001-7000 ( )

(ix) Rs.7001-8000 ( )

(x) Rs.8001-and above ( )

8. Land owned :

(i) No land ( )

(ii) Less than one acre ( )

(iii) 1 -- 5 acres ( )

(iv) 6 --10 acres ( )

(v) 11 -- 15 acres ( )

(vii) 21--50 acres ( )

(viii) 51 and above ( )

9. Type of House:

(i) No house ( )

(ii) Hut ( )

(iii) Katcha house ( )

(iv) Mixed house ( )

(v) Pucca house ( )

(vi) Mansion ( )

10. Social participation:

Are\Were you a member of any of the following institutions?

	Yes	No
1. Political	( )	( )
2. Panchayat	( )	( )
3. Co-operative	( )	( )
4. Educational	( )	( )
5. Welfare	( )	( )
6. Recreational	( )	( )
7. Caste	( )	( )
8. Religious	( )	( )
9. Any other (specify)	( )	( )

Appendix-II

THE LEVELS OF EXPOSURE TO MASS MEDIA AND CONTACT WITH EXTENSION AGENCIES

	Regularly	Occasionally	Very rarely	Never
1. How often do you read newspapers? (or do you make somebody to read)	( )	( )	( )	( )
2. How often do you listen Radio?	( )	( )	( )	( )
3. How often do you read Magazines?	( )	( )	( )	( )
4. How often do you see movies with regard to education, agriculture, health, family welfare *etc*.?	( )	( )	( )	( )
5. How often do you see T.V. programmes	( )	( )	( )	( )
6. How often do you attend agricultural demonstration classes?	( )	( )	( )	( )
7. How often do you attend lectures meetings, organized by politicians, social workers *etc*. in your village?	( )	( )	( )	( )

	Regu-larly	Occa-sionally	Very rarely	Never
8. How often do you meet the teachers of your village and discuss the school problems?	( )	( )	( )	( )
9. How often do you initiate discussion with your community members on the problems of developmental programmes in your village?	( )	( )	( )	( )
10. How often do you discuss with V.L.W.s. about agricultural operations and other developmental activities?	( )	( )	( )	( )
11. How often do you discuss with the village health visitors about health problems?	( )	( )	( )	( )
12. How often do you attend Taluq and District level meetings?	( )	( )	( )	( )
13. How often do you discuss with the rural development and extension services agencies?	( )	( )	( )	( )
14. How often do you discusses with Zilla Parishad and other high officials regarding the developmental problems?	( )	( )	( )	( )
15. How often do you discuss with different rural credit financial resources available?	( )	( )	( )	( )

Appendix-III

SCALE FOR MEASURING THE LEVELS OF ASPIRATIONS

Education, employment and income are important dimensions of social status of a person. Given an opportunity to rise in your social status how much education, income and political status, you aspire to attain for your success in life.

Education :

1. Primary ( )
2. Middle School ( )
3. High School ( )
4. Intermediate ( )
5. Graduation ( )
6. Professional/Post-Graduation ( )

Income :

1. Below Rs.1000 ( )
2. Rs.1001-2000 ( )
3. Rs.2001-3000 ( )
4. Rs.3001-4000 ( )
5. Rs.4001-5000 ( )
6. Rs.5001-6000 ( )

7. Rs.6001-7000 ( )
8. Rs.7001-8000 ( )
9. Rs.8001-9000 ( )
10. Rs.9001-and above ( )

Political Position:

1. One of the leader in the village ( )
2. Important leader in the village ( )
3. One of the leader in Taluk ( )
4. Important leader in Taluk ( )
5. One of the leader in District ( )
6. Important leader in District ( )
7. One of the leader in State ( )
8. Important leader in State ( )
9. One of the leader in Nation ( )
10. Important leader in Nation ( )

Appendix-IV

SOCIAL AWARENESS

't' ratio

I. 1. The traditional money-lenders were more helpful than the present day credit organizations. Do you agree? — 3.72**

(i) Agree ( )

(ii) Undecided ( )

(iii) Disagree ( )

2. Is it desirable to encourage people to approach the new credit institutions which have legal implications? — 3.29**

(i) Desirable ( )

(ii) Undecided ( )

(iii) Not desirable ( )

3. Is it ever possible to wean away people from traditional money-lenders? — 3.10**

(i) Possible ( )

(ii) Undecided ( )

(iii) Not possible ( )

II.1. Over anxiety for education is not called for because education does not necessarily make difference to the human quality? 3.24**

(i) Agree ( )

(ii) Undecided ( )

(iii) Disagree ( )

2. Is it desirable for the people to go in for education at any cost: 3.10**

(i) desirable ( )

(ii) undecided ( )

3. Is it ever possible to make every common man educated? 3.99**

(i) possible ( )

(ii) undecided ( )

(iii) not possible ( )

III.1. The villages were happier places to live in before the advent of the system of elections. Do you agree? 2.72**

(i) agree ( )

(ii) undecided ( )

(iii) disagree ( )

2. Is it desirable to continue with the system of elections however deficient they may be at the moment? 2.73**

(i) desirable ( )

ii) undecided ( )

(iii) not desirable ( )

3. Is it ever possible to cultivate faith in common man that the elections 3.72**

are the only way for the betterment of our society?

(i) possible ( )

(ii) undecided ( )

(iii) not possible ( )

IV.1. All men are not born equal hence social equality is an empty ideal. 2.1*

(i) agree

(ii) undecided

(iii) disagree

2. Is it desirable on the part of the weaker section to depend so much on government for their upliftment? 1.99*

(i) desirable ( )

(ii) undecided ( )

(iii) not desirable ( )

3. Is it ever possible to change the status of the weaker sections in our society? 2.2*

(i) possible ( )

(ii) undecided ( )

(iii) not possible ( )

V.1. Marriage of children is the private concern of the family, therefore there need not be any legal and special restrictions. Do you agree? 3.14**

(i) agree ( )

(ii) undecided ( )

(iii) disagree ( )

2. Is it desirable to ban child marriage legally? 2.61*

(i) desirable ( )

(ii) undecided ( )

(iii) not desirable ( )

3. Is it possible to ban child narriage in our society? 2.0*

(i) possible ( )

(ii) undecided ( )

(iii) not possible ( )

VI.1. Untouchability is practised in Hindu society which has its own advantages why should this practice be tampered with in the name of reform ? Do you agree? 3.29**

(i) agree ( )

(ii) undecided ( )

(iii) disagree ( )

2. Is it desirable to punish people who believe in untouchability which happens to be their traditions: 2.69**

(i) desirable ( )

(ii) undecided ( )

(iii) not desirable ( )

3. Is it ever possible to eliminate this practice from our society? 3.39**

(i) possible ( )

(ii) undecided ( )

(iii) not possible ( )

VII.1. Dowry is a part of financial adjustment of the family, and is based on the mutual advantage of the two parties. Do you agree? 1.99**

(i) agree ( )

(ii) undecided ( )

(iii) disagree ( )

2. Is it desirable to lay restriction on such private matters? 2.0*

(i) desirable ( )

(ii) undecided ( )

(iii) undesirable ( )

3. Is it ever possible to do away with the problem of dowry? 2.2*

(i) possible ( )

(ii) undecided ( )

(iii) not possible ( )

VIII.1. It is normal for children to work at home. Therefore children working out of home to support their family need not be viewed as an evil. Do you agree? 1.99*

(i) agree ( )

(ii) undecided ( )

(iii) disagree ( )

2. Is it desirable to ban child labour depriving some income to the poor parents? 2.72**

(i) desirable ( )

(ii) undecided ( )

(iii) not desirable ( )

3. Is it ever possible to do away with child labour in our society? 2.72**
   (i) possible ( )
   (ii) undecided ( )
   (iii) not possible ( )

IX.1. Daughters claiming equal share of property with the parents, only alienate them from their brothers. Do you agree? 3.23**
   (i) agree ( )
   (ii) undecided ( )
   (iii) disagree ( )

2. Is it desirable to disrupt the family by this legal fad? 3.26**
   (i) desirable ( )
   (ii) undecided ( )
   (iii) not desirable ( )

3. Is it possible to make female descendancy a reality in our society? 3.34**
   (i) possible ( )
   (ii) undecided ( )
   (iii) not possible ( )

X.1. Marriages are unbreakable bonds. No human hand should interfere with wedlock. Do you agree? 3.74**
   (i) agree ( )
   (ii) undecided ( )
   (iii) disagree ( )

2. Is it desirable for any one to have freedom to divorce his/her spouse in case of incompatibility? 2.34**

(i) desirable ( )

(ii) undecided ( )

(iii) not desirable ( )

3. Is it ever possible for women in our society to exercise this right? 2.3*

(i) possible ( )

(ii) undecided ( )

(iii) not possible ( )

XI.1. Land is meant for cultivation, no matter who own it as long as it is tilled to mutual best advantage of the tiller and owner. Do you agree? 4.21**

(i) agree ( )

(ii) undecided ( )

(iii) disagree ( )

2. Is it desirable to dispossess the owner of the land to give it over to the tiller? 2.32*

(i) desirable ( )

(ii) undecided ( )

(iii) not desirable ( )

3. Is it ever possible to implement the land ceiling act successfully? 2.73*

(i) possible ( )

(ii) undecided ( )

(iii) not possible ( )

XII.1. The tensions between the employer and employee is unwanted situation. Mutual adjustment between themselves will lead to better human relations. Do you agree? 3.59**

(i) agree ( )

(ii) undecided ( )

(iii) disagree ( )

2. Is it desirable to create opposite plans between employer and employee by designing terms and conditions between the two through legal acts? 3.34**

(i) desirable ( )

(ii) undecided ( )

(iii) not desirable ( )

3. Is it ever possible to eliminate the exploitation of employee by the employer through legal means? 2.34*

(i) possible ( )

(ii) undecided ( )

(iii) not possible ( )

XIII.1. Although it is true that union is strength, to use it against one's own master is sinful. Do you agree? 3.34**

(i) agree ( )

(ii) undecided ( )

(iii) disagree ( )

2. Is it desirable to organise such labour unions at the cost of peace and harmony in our society? 2.34*

(i) desirable ( )

(ii) undecided ( )

(ii) not desirable ( )

3. Is it ever possible to do away with the exploitation of masters in our society? 3.74**

i) possible ( )

ii) undecided ( )

iii) not possible ( )

XIV.1.Many feel that voting is an unnecessary waste of time as no one votes with his conscience. Do you agree? 4.32*

(i) agree ( )

(ii) undecided ( )

(iii) disagree ( )

2. Is it desirable to make voting legally compulsory? 2.23**

(i) desirable ( )

(ii) undecided ( )

(iii) not desirable ( )

3. Is it ever possible to eliminate apathy for voting in our society? 3.2**

(i) possible ( )

(ii) decided ( )

(iii) not possible ( )

'**t**' **ratio**

XV.1.To talk of self employment is to talk of no 3.74**

employment, at all. Do you agree?

(i) agree ( )

(ii) undecided ( )

(iii) disagree ( )

2. Is it desirable to young man to risk their career in the name of self-employment? 3.32**

(i) desirable ( )

(ii) undecided ( )

(iii) not desirable ( )

3. Is it ever possible to eliminate the conditions which obstruct risk taking behaviour of the young for independent enterprise? 3.34**

(i) possible ( )

(ii) undecided ( )

(iii) not possible ( )

XVI.1.Marriages are meant for progeny and the number of children to that one should have is a personal matter? Do you agree? 3.34**

(i) agree ( )

(ii) undecided ( )

(iii) disagree ( )

2. Is it desirable to plan and control number of children interfering with the plans of God? . 3.74**

(i) desirable ( )

(ii) undecided ( )

(iii) not desirable ( )

3. Is it ever possible to eliminate traditional respect 3.32**

for large family?

(i) possible ( )

(ii) undecided ( )

(iii) not possible ( )

XVII.1. We had better indigenous medicines to cure even deadly diseases? Do you agree? 4.32**

(i) agree ( )

(ii) undecided ( )

(iii) disagree ( )

2. Is it desirable to encourage people to rely on the modern medicines? 4.38**

(i) desirable ( )

(ii) undecided ( )

(iii) not desirable ( )

3. Is it ever possible to create faith in our people that modern medicines are based on scientific approach? 3.74**

(i) possible ( )

(ii) undecided ( )

(iii) not possible ( )

XVIII.1. We had better approaches to solve our health problems by virtue of our faith in Guru and deity than what the present doctors can do for us? Do you agree? 3.59**

(i) agree ( )

(ii) undecided ( )

't' ratio

(iii) disagree ( )

2. Is it desirable to root out such age-old faith which has been a great source for healing of number of diseasess? 3.34*

   (i) desirable ( )

   (ii) undecided ( )

   (iii) not desirable ( )

3. Is it ever possible to do away with the superstitions in our society? 3.59**

   (i) possible ( )

   (ii) undecided ( )

   (iii) not possible ( )

* Significant = .05 level.

** Significant =.01 level.

Appendix-V

SCALE TO MEASURE DEMOCRATIC VS. AUTHORITARIAN LEADERSHIP

<u>'t' ratio</u>

1. In a move to start a co-operative market in your village, the people are divided on this issue and your group is opposed to starting the market. What would be your reaction? — 2.92**

   (i) Support the stand taken by your group ( )

   (ii) Explain to your group the advantages of starting a cooperative market ( )

   (iii) Oppose the views of your group and boycott it if not convinced ( )

2. In a dispute among your village for selecting a site for a village clinic you are expected to play a major role in finalising the site. What criteria would you adopt in selecting such a site? — 2.69**

   (i) Ignore them as majority of villagers are ignorant ( )

   (ii) Take their suggestions but finally go according to your views ( )

   (iii) Act according to the majority's opinon ( )

3. In a family planning programme organized for your village, many old people are opposed to the programme. What would be your stand in the situation? 2.35**

   (i) Accept the views of the old people as they are more experienced ( )

   (ii) Try to convince them and give it up if they still oppose ( )

   (iii) Go all out for the implementation of the programme ( )

4. In a scheme to promote youth clubs in your district the authorities turn down your application without subscribing any reason. What would be your general action? 3.27**

   (i) Accept this because decision of the authoritiesshould be respected. ( )

   (ii) Represent for reconsideration and give it if not possible ( )

   (iii) Insist on knowing the reasons for rejection and protest if reasons are not convincing ( )

5. If Zamindar of your village makes a statement about his employee which according to you is offensive, what would be your normal reaction? 4.78**

   (i) Accept it as this is normal in our society ( )

   (ii) Express your resentment ( )

   (iii) Demand an apology from the Zamindar ( )

6. Suppose you have been repeatedly told by your followers about the exploitation of poor by a few rich elders of the village. What would be your usual reaction? 3.68**

   (i) Take it as normal in our society ( )

(ii) Try to educate such people for changing their ways of treating the employees ( )

(iii) Expose them ( )

7. When you happen to be in a group of people who are all strangers to you, what is your normal behaviour? 3.82**

(i) You take initiative to talk to them ( )

(ii) Wait and respond according to their initiative ( )

(iii) Maintain distance as far as possible ( )

8. When some people go on bothering you narrating their problems what is your usual reaction? 6.19**

(i) Discourage them from bothering you ( )

(ii) Tolerate them as this is a necessary evil ( )

(iii) Listen to them sympathetically ( )

9. You find some people criticising you whenever you fail in your attempts. Do you normally? 4.72**

(i) Give them a bit of your mind ( )

(ii) Be indifferent as this is meaningless ( )

(iii) Accept the criticism and try to improve yourself ( )

10. In a situation which you can handle with confidence you find some of your friends offering their suggestions for handling it better, what is your normal reaction? 5.90**

(i) Snub them as their suggestions are unwanted ( )

(ii) Listen to their point of view but have your own way

(iii) Take the suggestions with an open mind ( )

11. In spite of the fact that you take maximum trouble to explain a point to a person who comes to you for advice, he insists on further clarification what is your usual behaviour in such situation? 6.32**

(i) You get annoyed ( )

(ii) You sympathise but feel helpless ( )

(iii) You make it a point to explain to the person till he understands ( )

12. If the bank authorities refuse to advance loan to one of your villagers for which he is entitled what is your customary reaction? 3.78**

(i) Accept it as this is one of the usual matters ( )

(ii) To take initiative and appeal for reconsideration ( )

(iii) Carry on a campaign against the bank authorites ( )

13. You find that your son's name is struck off the rolls of the school for his irregularity. What will be your usual reaction? 3.72**

(i) Consider it as a damage to your prestige therefore threaten the school authorities ( )

(ii) Use your good offices and seek readmission ( )

(iii) Respect the decision of the authorities and proceed according to the rules ( )

14. Suppose you are trying to meet your higher authorities to represent your important problem, even after your repeated attempts you are not given an appointment, what would be your reaction? 4.12**

(i) You accept it as authorities should not be questioned ( )

(ii) Feel annoyed ( )

(iii) Bring pressure on the authority to receive your representation. ( )

15. At a reception arranged in a village for the collector of your district, you want to meet the collector, somebody prevents you from meeting the collector. Whether your customary reaction is: 2.73**

(i) To do nothing as a mark of respect to the authority ( )

(ii) To enter into an argument ( )

(iii) To create a scene and insist on meeting the collector ( )

16. One of your close relatives who is an important officer in your district is proved to be corruptive and there is a protest from public against him. What is your usual reaction? 3.79**

(i) Use your influence and protect the officer ( )

(ii) Maintain silence, not to take sides ( )

(iii) Be a party for the dismissal of the officer ( )

17. If one of the very honest persons of your village is punished by village 'pedda'on an allegation which according to you is baseless. What would be your reaction? 3.76**

(i) Respect the action taken by 'pedda' as village, 'pedda' should not be questioned ( )

(ii) Ignore this as it is difficult to protest against 'pedda' ( )

(iii) Initiate protest against 'pedda' ( )

18. You find that due to the stand taken by a member in a committee meeting your proposals are likely to be rejected by the committee. Do you then: 2.38**

(i) Boycott the group as this is humiliating ( )

(ii) Maintain silence ( )

(iii) Accept the group decision ( )

19. You find members of your group claiming false credit for the success of your group in an election, which according to you would have been defeated but for your crucial role. Do you them: 4.12**

(i) Snub the members ( )

(ii) Ignore them to avoid unpleasantness ( )

(iii) Share their excitement as this is the success of the entire gruop ( )

20. In an election in which you have taken part, some member grade you with low credits in comparison to others who are working with you. How do you react generally in such situations? 2.10*

(i) Quit the group with potest ( )

(ii) React at the comparison with protest ( )

(iii) Welcome the comparison ( )

21. In an election for Panchayat Board your group is likely to be defeated. What would be your customary reaction? 3.46**

(i) Try to sabotage the whole thing ( )

(ii) Be indifferent ( )

(iii) Make all best efforts to mobilise the public opinion in favour of your group and leave the rest to the decision of the electorate. ( )

22. If the president of Panchayat Samithi insults you by virtue of his position. What would be your reaction? 3.22**

    (i) Accept the situation as the people occupying higher positions have to be respected. ( )

    (ii) Enter into discussion ( )

    (iii) Create a scene and expose him ( )

23. If the leader of your group becomes a tool in the hands of the authorities and betrays the casue for which he is elected. What would be your reaction? 3.79**

    (i) Be blind to the mistakes of the leader ( )

    (ii) Warn the leader with consequence ( )

    (iii) Organise no-confidence motion ( )

24. You find that a member of your group is penalised for an offence committed by you, the secret of this is not known to anyone except you. What is your normal reaction? 3.79**

    (i) Wise enough to be silent ( )

    (ii) Apologise the member privately expressing your guilt ( )

    (iii) Confess your offence publicly ( )

25. If you come across a situation which you find that distribution of subsidiary loans are made by favouritism (Like caste and regional feelings) and deserving persons are deprived of their legitimate chances. Do you usually? 2.73**

    (i) Accept the situation as this is normal in your society ( )

(ii) Express your concern publicly ( )

(iii) Organise a mass protest ( )

26. It is said that landlords in general manipulate the records to escape from the ceiling act. How do you react to this? 3.21**

(i) Ignore it as land belongs to them for decades ( )

<u>'t' ratio</u>

(ii) Organise public opinion to eliminate such manipulation ( )

(iii) Take up the matter with higher authorities and expose the landlords ( )

27. At a ceremonial ritual like Dussehra day in your village, a person belonging to the lower caste takes front seats available, and organisers object saying they are meant for upper class people. What would be your reaction? 5.90**

(i) Accept the arrangements as this goes with our tradition. ( )

(ii) Enter into the argument with the organisers ( )

(iii) Provoke the lower class people and help them in occupying the front chairs ( )

28. You are interested in organising an agitation against the evils of untouchability in your village and all your people oppose you. Do you in that situation? 3.79**

(i) Give up the idea as it is always better to obey the elders. ( )

(ii) Persuade them and give up the idea if they still oppose you. ( )

(iii) Start the agitation in spite of their disapproval ( )

29. Suppose you go to a cinema in which you are extremely interested and find a big queue at the ticket counter. What would you normally do? 5.34**

(i) Not mind to buy the ticket in black market rather than standing in queue ( )

(ii) Go back with disappointment ( )

(iii) Stand in the queue and wait for your turn to buy the ticket. ( )

30. When you find that one of your neighbours is a wife beater and always ill-treates his wife. What would be your customary reaction to him? 4.78**

(i) Not to interfere with the situation as this is a private affair. ( )

(ii) Warn your neighbour with consequence ( )

(iii) To persuade thc lady to divorce her husband if it is not possible to change his behaviour ( )

* Significant at .05 level.

** Significant at .01 level.

Bibliography

Abida Samiuddin, "The Emerging Pattern of Rural Leadership", *Kurukshetra*, February 1977.

Airan J.W., (1969)(ed), *The Nature of Leadership*, (Bombay: Lalvani Publishing House).

Ansari A., "Value Orientation Scale", Department of Psychology, Aligarh Muslim University, in *Hand Book of Psychological and Sociological Instruments*, edited by Pareek and Venkateswara Rao, (Ahmedabad: Sahitya Mudranalayam).

Asthana, B.C., "Kshetra Pramukhs - The Emerging Leaders", *Kurukshetra*, 15, No.8 (May, 1967).

Atal Yogesh, (1971) *Local Communities and National Politics*, Part-III, (Delhi: National).

Bachenheimer R., "Elements of Leadership in an Andhra Village". In *Leadership and Political Institutions in India*, edited by Park and Tinker, (Princeton: N.J.Princeton University Press, 1959).

Bada C.R. "Village Panchayat Key leadership Pattern", *Interdiscipline*, Vol. 12, No. 12, (1975).

_______ *The Study of Voting Behaviour in Gulbarga District*, (Gulbarga: The Institute of Vichar Bharati Adyayana Vedike, 1974).

Barth, Ernest, A.T., and Johnson, Stuart, D., "Community Power and a Typology of Social Issues", *Social Forces*, Vol. 38, (October - 1959).

Bass, Bernard M., (1960) *Leadership, Psychology and Organizational Behaviour*, (New York: Harper and Row).

Beals Alan., "Change in Leadership of a Mysore Village". In *Rural*

Sociology in India edited by A.R.Desai, (Bombay: The Indian Society of Agricultural Economics, 1978).

Bendix, Reinhard, (1967) *Tradition and Modernity Reconsidered* Comparative Studies in Society and History.

Beteille, Andre, (1966) *Caste Old and New - Essays in Social Structure and Social Stratification*, (Bombay: University of Bombay).

_______*Caste, Class and Power - Changing Patterns of Stratification in Tanjore Village*, (Bombay: Oxford University Press, 1966).

Bhatt, K.S., *Panchayat Raj in Mysore*, Unpublished Ph.D. Thesis, (Bombay: University of Bombay, 1966).

_______"Emerging Pattern of Leadership in Panchayat Raj set-up in Mysore State". In *Readings on Panchayat Raj*, edited by Jacob, George, (Hyderabad: N.I.C.D., 1967).

Bhouskar, K.M., "Leadership in a Tribal Village", *Man in India*, 44, No.4, (October-December, 1964).

Blalock Hubert, (1960) M., *Social Statistics*, (New York: McGraw Hill Book Company, Inc.,).

Blumer, Herbert., "Industrialization and Traditional Order", *Sociology and Social Research*, 48, (1964).

Bonjean, C.M., and Oslon David, M., "Community Leadership". In *Perspectives on the American Community* edited by Ronald L. Warren, (Chicago: Rand McNally and Co., 1966).

_______"Community Leadership - Directions of Research", *Administrative Science Quarterly*, Vol. 9, No.3, (October, 1964).

Borgardus, Emory.S., (1934) *Leaders and Leadership*, (New York: Appleton Century Crofts, INC.).

Bose, A.B., and Malhotra, S.P., "Some Characters of Occupational Castes in Central and Lower Luni in Western Rajasthan", *Eastern Anthropologist*, 17.

Cassels's, Level of Aspiration Test, cited in S.B. Red, J.L.McCary, Bette, Johnson, "A Study of Relationship between Aspirational Levels and Academic Achievements", *The Journal of Educational Research*, Vol.55, No.4, (December-January, 1962).

Cantril, Hadley, *The Pattern of Human Concerns*, (New Brunswick, N.J.Rutgers University Press, 1965).

Chandra, Prabhat, "Rural Leadership in India", *The Eastern Anthropologist*, 12, (September - November, 1959).

Chaudhri, Ranjit, "Pattern of Village Leadership in a West Bengal Village", *Economic Weekly*, 16, No.14, (April 4, 1964).

Chauhan, B.R., (1968), "Phases in Village Power Structure and Leadership in Rajasthan". In *Leadership in India*, edited by Vidyarthi L.P., (Bombay: Asia Publishing House).

Clark, Terry N., (1968) (ed), *Community Structure and Decision Making - Comparative Analysis*, (San Francisco. Chandler Publishing Co.).

Cronback, Lee J., (1961) *Educational Psychology*, (London: Stapler Press).

Dahl, Robert, A., (1958) "A Critique of the Ruling Elite Model". *American Political Science Review*, Vol. 52, (June).

Darwin, Cartwright and Alvin Zander (ed), (1956) Group Dynamics: *Research and Theory*, (Evanston, Illinois, Rowpeterson Co.).

Dasgupta, S., "Patterns of Agricultural Leadership and Innovation in Six Indian villages", *Indian Journal of Extension Education*, Vol.1 (4), (1966).

Desai, A.R., (1978) *Rural Sociology in India*, (Bombay: Popular Prakashan).

De Sola Pool, Ithiel., "The Role of Communication in the Process of Modernization and Technological Change". In *Industrialization and Society* edited by Bert. F. Hoselitz and Wilbert, E. Moore, (The Hague: UNESCO-Mouton, 1963).

______"The Mass India and Their Interpersonal Social Functions in the Porcess of Modernization". In *Society and Mass Communication* edited by Dexter and White, (Glenco, Free Press, 1954).

Deutsch, Karl W., "Social Mobilization and Political Development", *American Political Review*, Vol. IV, No.3, (September, 1961).

Dhillon, H.S., (1955) *Leadership and Groups in a South Indian Village*, (New Delhi, Planning Commission, P.E.O. Publications, No.9).

Dube, Leela., "Leadership in C.D. and Decentralized Democracy", *Kurukshetra*, 14, No.9 (June - 1966).

______"Studies of Leadership in Village India", *Emerging Patterns of Rural Leadership in Southern Asia*, (Hyderabad: N.I.C.D. 1965).

Dube, S.C., "Frame-work for the Study of Rural Leadership in Transitional Societies". In *Emerging Patterns of Rural Leadership in Southern Asia*, edited by Leela Dube., (Hyderabad: N.I.C.D. 1965).

______"Caste Dominance and Factionalism", *Contribution to Indian Sociology*, New Series, 2, (December, 1968).

______"Dominant Caste and Village Leadership", Paper presented at Seminar on Trends of change in Village India, Mussoorie, (N.I.C.D., 1961).

______"Foreword", *Leadership in India* edited by Vidyarthi, L.P. (Bombay: Asia Publishing House, 1968).

______*Indian Village*, (New York: Harper and Row, 1967).

______"Modernization and its Adaptive Demands on Indian Society". In *Papers in the Sociology of Education in India*, edited by Gore, M.S., and others, (Delhi: NCERT, 1967).

______"Ranking of Castes in Telangana Village", *Eastern Anthropologist*, 8, (324).

Edgar, Dale, "Introduction" *to Mass - Media and Education, The Fifty Third Year Book of the National Society for the Study of Education*, edited by Henry, Nelson B., (Illinois, NSSE, 1954).

Ehrlich, Howard J., "Power and Democracy: A Critical Discussion". In *Power and Democracy in America*, edited by William V.D. Antonio and Howard J., Ehrlich, (Notre Dame, Indiana: University of Notre Dame Press, 1961).

______"The Reputational Approach to the Study of Community Power", *American Sociological Review*, Vol.26, (December, 1961).

Elder, Joseph W., "Caste and World-View - The Application of Survey Research Methods". In *Structure and Change in Indian Society*, edited by Milton Singer and Bernard S.Cohn, (Chicago: Aldine Publishing Company, 1968).

Fairchild, H.P., (1967) *Dictionary of Sociology*, (Totowa: N.J. Little Field Adms & Co.).

Filella, S.J.,(1969). "The Psychology of Leadership". In *The Nature of Leadership - A Practical Approach*, edited by Airan, J.W., (Bombay: Lalvani Publishing House).

Fisher, S., "Community - Power Studies: A Critique", *Social Research*, Vol. 29, No.4 (Winter - 192).

Fliegal, Frederick C., and others, *Agricultural Innovations in Indian Village*, (Hyderabad: N.I.C.D., 1968).

Form, William. H., and Sanes, Wanen L., "Organized Labour's Image of Community Power Structure", *Social Forces*, Vol. 38 (May - 1966).

Form, William H., and Antonio, William, V.D., "Integration and cleavage Among Community Influentials in Two Border cities", *American Sociological Review*, Vol. 25 (December, 1959).

Francis; Abraham M., *Dynamics of Leadership in Village India*. (Allahbad: Indian International Publication, 1974).

______"Studies in Leadership: A critique on Empirical and Conceptual Analysis", *The Indian Journal of Social Work*, (Bombay: Tata Institute Vol.XXXIII, No.3, October, 1972).

Frankle, Francine R., (1971) *India's Green Revolution*, (Princeton University Press).

Franklin, Fearing, "Social Impact of the Mass Media of Communication". In *Mass Media and Education - The Fifty Third Year Book of the National Society for the Study of Education*, edited by Henry, Nelson B., (Illinois, NSSE, 1954).

Freeman, Frank S., (1960) *Theory and Practice of Psychological Testing*, (Holt Reinehart and Winston, Inc. New York).

Gangrade K.D., (1974). *Emerging Pattern of Leadership*, (Rachana Publications).

_______"Panchayat Elections and Leadership: A caste Study". In *Studies in Rural Leadership*, edited by Udai Pareek (Delhi: Behavioural Science Centre, 1966).

Ghurye, G.S., *Caste Class and Occupation* (Bombay: Popular Book Depot).

Gibb, Cecil A., "Leadership", *International Encyclopedia of Social Sciences*, edited by David L. Shills, (New York: The Macmillan Company and The Free Press, 1968).

_______"Leadership". In *Hand Book of Social Psychology*, edited by Gardner, Lindsey, Vol.II, (London: Addison-Wesley Publishing Company Inc., 1959).

_______The Principles and Traits of Leadership", *Journal of Abnormal and Social Psychology*, Vol. XIII, (July, 1947).

Gouldner, Alvin., (ed),(1950) *Studies in Leadership*, (New York: Harper and Brothers).

Gupta, L.C., "Changing Pattern of Rural Leadership - A case Study", *Sociological Bulletin*, 15, No.2, (September, 1966).

Gupta, Raghuraj., (1966) *Decision Makers in a Gramdan Village* (Lucknow: Planning Research and Action Institute).

Guruswamy M.P., "Local Leadership in Rural Development", *Khadi Gramodyog*, (Bombay: August, 1960).

G.W. and F.H. All Port "The All Port - A.S. Reaction Study", (Houghton Mifflin Co., 1928-29).

Haiman, Frankly, *Group Leadership and Democratic Action*, (Massachusetts, Houghton Mifflin, Co., 1951).

Haller, A.O., "On the Concept of Aspirations", *Rural Sociology*, 33(4), (1968).

Harper, Edward, B., Harper, Louise G., "Political Organization and Leadership in a Karnataka Village". In *Leadership and Political Institutions in India*, edited by Park and Tinkers, (Princeton N.J., Princeton University Press, 1959).

Hitchock, John T., "Leadership in a North Indian Village: Two case Studies". In *Leadership and Political Institutions in India*, edited by Park and Tinker, (Princeton: Princeton University Press, 1959).

Hollander, E.P., (1963). *Leaders, Groups and Influence*, (New York: Oxford University Press).

Homans, George C., (1950). *The Job of the Leader : The Human Group*, (New York: Harcourt Brace and World, Inc.).

Hunter, Floyd, (1963). *Community Power Structure - A Study of Decision Makers*, (Garden City, New York: Doubleday).

Illich, Ivan, (1977). *Deschooling Society*, (New York: Madison Avenue, Penguin Books).

Inamdar, N.A., (1970). *Functions of Village Panchayats*, (Bombay: Popular Prakashan).

Ingalls, Daniel, "The Brahmin Tradition". In *Traditional India - Structure and Change*, edited by Singer, Milton, (Philadelphia; American Folklore Society, 1959).

Inkels, Alex, "Making Men Modern: On the cause and consequences of Individual change in six Developing Countries", *American Journal of Sociology*, Vol.75, No.2, (1969).

Ishwaran, K., (ed), (1970). *Change and Continuity in India's Villages*,

(Columbia University Press).

Jacob, George, (ed), (1967). *Readings on Panchayat Raj*, (Hyderabad, N.I.C.D.).

Jadeja Y.D., "Trends in Village Leadership in Three Villages of Gujarat", *Khadigramodyog*, 10, No.9, (June - 1964).

Jain,S.C.. *Community Development and Panchayat Raj in India*, (Delhi: Allied Publishers, 1967).

Jaya Krishna Baral, "Leadership and Factionalism in Indian Villages", *Journal of Socio and Economic Studies*, 5, (2), (September, 1975).

Kanungo, S.C. *et al*. "Perception of Leadership roles in Rural Setting", *Studies in Rural Leadership* edited by Udai Pareek, (Delhi: Behavioural Sciences Centre, 1966).

Karani R.N., "Leadership for Democracy". In *The Nature of Leadership - A Practical Approach* edited by Airan, J.W., (Bombay: Lalvani Publishing House, 1969).

Karipurath, Paul, *The Emerging Patterns of Leadership in Mysore State*, (Mysore: Administrative Training Institute).

Katz E. and Lazarsfeld, P.F., (1960). Personal Influence, *The Part Played by people in the flow of Mass Communication*, (New York, The Free Press).

Kilpatrick, F.P. and H. Cantril, "Self-anchoring scaling: A Measure of Individuals' Unique reality worlds", *Journal of Individual Psychology*, (1960).

Kothari, Rajni, (1970). *Politics in India*, (Boston Little Brown and Company).

Kretch D. and Crutch Field, R.S., (1948). *Theory and Problems of Social Psychology*, (New York: McGraw Hill Book Co.).

Kretch D. *et al*., (1962). *Individual in Society*, (New York: McGraw Hill Book Co., Inc.).

Kuppu Swamy, B., (1934). "A Scale to Measure Socio-Economic Status", *Indian Journal of Psychology*, Vol. 34.

K.R.Reddy, *Value Pattern and Vocational Sense Among High School Students*, (Ph.D. Thesis submitted to Osmania University, 1971).

Lasswell, Harold D., "The structure and function of Communication in society". In *The Communication of India* edited by Bryson, Lyman, (New York: Harper and Row, 1948).

Lasswell, Harold D. *et al.*, (ed) (1965). *Language of Politics: Studies in Quantitative Semantics* (The M.I.T. Press).

--------*The Comparative Study of Elites*, (Palo Alto, California, Stanford University Press, 1952).

Lewis, Oscar (1958). *Village Life in North India*, (Urbana: University of Illinois Press, 1958).

"Group Dynamics in a North Indian Village" (Delhi, Planning Commission, P.E.O., 1954).

Lippit Ronald, *An experimental study of Authoritarian and democratic Group Atmosphere*, (University of Iowa Studies for child welfare, 1939).

---------- , and White Ralph, "Leader Behaviour and Member Reaction in Three Social climates". In *Group Dynamics*, edited by Cart Wright and Alvinzander, (New York: Harper and Row).

Lippit, Ronald, White Ralph, K., Lewin Kurt, "Pattern of Aggressive behaviour in experimentally created social climates". In *Leader Behaviour Description*, edited by Uemphill J.K., and Coones A.E., (Columbus, Ohio, Personnel Research Board, The Ohio State University, 1950).

Majumdar, D.N. (1958). *Caste and Communication in an Indian Village*, (Bombay: Asia Publishing House).

Malla Reddy, M., *A Few Selected Socio-Psychological Correlates of Student Activism, Unpublished Ph.D. thesis*, submitted to Osmania University, (Hydrabad, 1973).

Mathur J.C., and Neurath (1955). *An Indian Experiment in Farm Radio Forums*, (UNESCO).

McClelland, David C., (1961). *The Achieving Society*, (Princeton, New Jersey D'ven Nostrand Company, Inc.).

McCormack, William, "Factionalism in a Mysore Village". In, *Leadership and Political Institutions in India*, (ed) Park and Tinker (Princeton: Princeton University Press, 1959).

Mehata, S.R., (1972). *Emerging Pattern ofRural Leadership*, (Bombay: Wiley).

Mehata Uday, "The Impact of the Panchayat Raj on Rural India". In *Rural Sociology in India*, edited by A.R.Desai, 5th Edition, (Bombay: Popular Prakashan, 1978).

Miller, Delbert C., "Industry and Community Power Structure - A comparative study of an American and English City", *American Sociological Review*, Vol. 23, (February, 1958).

Mishra, S.N., "Emerging Leadership in Rural India - A Case Study", *Quarterly Journal of The Local Self-Government Institution*, Vol. XVII, No.2, (October-December, 1976).

"A Motivational Study of Role Responsibility," *Social Scientist*, 4(18) (March, 1976).

Muttayya, B.C., "Elected Village Leaders of India - A Psychological Analysis", *Behavioural Science and Community*, (1971, 5(1)).

--------"Leadership in Panchayats", *Community Development and Panchayat Raj Digest*, (1976, 7(4)).

--------"Personality and Value Orientation of Panchayat Leaders, Informal Leaders, and non-leaders: A Comparative Study," *Behavioural Sciences and Community Development*, Vol. 11, No.1, (March, 1977).

--------"Psycho-Social Study of Panchayat Leaders in Tamil Nadu", *Research Project* at (N.I.C.D., Hyderabad).

--------and Neeladri Raju K., "Personal and Social Background of Elected Village Leaders", Community Development and *Panchayat Raj Digest*, Vol.4, No.3, (January - 1973).

Nair S.P., "Leadership in Kerala Panchayats", *Khadi Gramodyog*, B.No.10, (July 1967).

Narain, Iqbal, "Democratic Decentralization and Rural Leadership in India, Rajasthan Experiment", *Asian Survey* Vol.IV, No.8, (1964).

--------K.C. Pande, Mohan Lal Sarma, (1976).*The Rural Elite in An Indian State - A Case Study in Rajasthan* (Delhi: Manohar Book Service).

Neeladri Raju, "The Emerging Elite in Rural India - A comparative Study of Elites in A.P., Maharashtra, and West Bengal", *Behavioural Sciences and Community Development*, Vol.5, No.1 (March, 1972).

Nirmalkantisaha, "Leadership and Adoption of Agricultural Innovations", Kurukshetra - *Journal of Community Development and Village Democracy*, (January 1, 1975).

N.Y. Reddy, "*Adolescent Adjustment in Relation to Home environment*, Unpublished Ph.D. Thesis submitted to Osmania University (1966).

Oomen T.K., "Rural Community power structure in India", *Social Forces*, 49(2), (1970).

Opler, Morris E., "Factors of Tradition and change in a Local Election in Rural India". In *Leadership and Political Institutions in India*, edited by Park and Tinker, (Princeton, Princeton University Press, 1959).

Ordway Tead (1963). *The Art of Leadership*, (New York: McGraw Hill Book Co.).

"Trends of Change in Village India", *Kurukshetra*, Ministry of Community Development, (New Delhi, 1962).

Orenstein A., "Leadership and Caste in a Bombay Village". In *Leadership and Political Institutions in India*, edited by Park and Tinker, (Princeton, Princeton University Press, 1959).

Pai Panandikar, "Development Administration - An Approach", *The Indian Journal of Public Administration*, Vol.X, No.1, (January - March, 1964).

Pande B.K., and Jain P.N., "Rural Leadership - Differentials in Emerging Pattern", *Kurukshetra*, 14, No.4 (January, 1966).

Pandya, Hiren J., "Development Administration and Rural Leadership in India", *Social Change*, Vol.5, No.3&4, (September -December, 1975).

Pareek, Udai, (ed.), *Studies in Rural Leadership*, (Delhi: Behavioural Sciences Centre, (1966).

--------*et al.*, "Behavioural Characteristics of Effective Village Leaders as Reported by Non-Leader Farmers". In *Studies in Rural Leadership*, edited by Pareek, Udai, (Delhi: Behavioural Sciences Centre, 1966).

Pareek, U. and Trivedi, G., "Reliability and Validity of a rural Socio-Economic Status Scale", *Indian Journal of Applied Psychology*, 1(1), (1964).

Park, Richard L., and Irene, Tinker (1959). *Leadership and Political Institutions in India*, (Princeton, New Jersey: Princeton University Press,).

Parsons, Talcott, (1951). *The Social System* (New York: Free Press).

and Shills, A. Edward, (1952), *Towards a General Theory of Action*, (Cambridge: Harvard University Press,).

Patnaik, N. "Caste and Occupation in Rural Policy". In *Man in India*, 34.

Paul, Pigors, (1955) *Leadership of Domination*, (Boston, Houghton, Mifflin, Co.,).

Paulo, Freire, (1977). *Cultural Action for Freedom*, (England: Penguin Books Ltd.).

"Cultural Freedom in Latin America". In *Human Rights and the Liberation of Man in the America*, edited by Louis M. Colonese, (Indiana: University of Notre Dame Press, 1970).

--------(1975), *Pedagogy of the Oppressed*, (England, Penguin Books Ltd.).

Preston, M.G., and Bayton, J.A., "Differential effect of a Social Variable upon three levels of aspirations", *Journal of Experimental Psychology* (1941, 29).

Radhukar, W.D., "A scale for Measuring Socio-Economic Status of Indian Farm Families", *Nagpur Agriculture College Magazine*.

Ram Reddy G. and Seshadri K., (1972)*The Voter and Panchayat Raj - A Study of the Electoral Behaviour During Panchayat Elections in Warangal District, Andhra Pradesh*, (Hyderabad, N.I.C.D.).

Ranga Rao K., " Leadership in a Community Development Village". In *Sociological Aspects of Community Development*, edited by Moorthy, M.V., (Andhra University, Waltair, 1966).

"Rural Leadership and Conflict - A Study of an Andhra Village", *Economic and Political Weekly*, Vol. III, No. 17 (1968).

Robert Edgger, and Daniel, Goldrich, "Community Power Structure and Partisanship", *American Sociological Review*, Vol.23, (August-1958).

Robert Presthees, (1964). *Men At the Top - A Study in Community Power Network* (Oxford University Press,).

Rogers, Evert M., (1969). *Diffusion of Innovation - Modernization among Peasants - The Impact of Communication*, (New York: Reinehart and Winston, Inc.).

Ross, Murray G., and Hendry, Charles E., (1957). *New Understanding of Leadership - A Survey and application of Research*, (New York Association Press).

Rossi, Peter H., (1957). "Community Decision Making", *Administrative Science Quarterly*, Vol.1 (March).

Rossi, Peter H., Biddle, Bruce J., "Educational Media - Education and Society". In *the New Media and Education - Their Impact on Society*, edited by Rossi, Peter H., and Biddle, Bruce J., (New York: Anchor Books, Doubleday and Company, Inc. 1966).

Roy, Pradipto, (1967). "Emerging Pattern of Rural Leadership". In *Leadership in India*, edited by Vidyarthi L.P., (Bombay: Asia Publishing House).

"Participation in New Social Structure and Leadership". In *Emerging Patterns of Rural Leadership in Southern Asia*, edited by Dube, Leela, (Hyderabad, N.I.C.D., 1965).

--------and Sen, Lalit K., *Awareness of Community Development in Village India - A Preliminary Report*, (Hyderabad: NICD 1965).

Rout, B., "Rural Leadership Problems", *Kurukshetra*, 15, No.5 (February, 1967).

Sahay, B.N., "Village Leaders and Development Programme," *Khadigramodyog*, 13, No.7 (April-1967).

Salvi, P.V., and Patil R.Y., "Rural Local Leadership", *Rural India*, 31, No.9, (November 1968).

Saran, Paramatma, (1978). *Rural Leadership in the Context of India's Modernization*, (Vikas Publishing House Pvt. Ltd.).

Schnudrit, Richard, "Leadership". In *Encyclopedia of Social Sciences*, edited by Edwin R.A., Sehigman, Vol.IX-X (1957).

Sen Lalit K., (1961). *Opinion Leadership in India - A Study of Interpersonal Communication in Eight Villages*, (Hyderabad: N.I.C.D.).

SeWell W.H., and Shah V.P., "Social Class, Parental encouragement and educational Aspirations", *American Journal of Sociology*, (1968).

Shah, V.P. *et al*, "Social Class and Educational Aspirations in an Indian Metropolis", *Sociological Bulletin*, Vol. XX No. 2 (September 1971).

Singer Milton (ed.), (1959), *Traditional India: Structure and Change*, (Philadelphia: American Folk-lore Society).

Singh, A., (1973). *Leadership Pattern and Village Structure - A Case Study of Six Indian Villages*, (New Delhi: Sterling Publishers Pvt. Ltd.,).

Singh, B.N., "The Impact of the Community Development Programme on Rural Leadership". In *Leadership and Political Institutions in India*, edited by Park and Tinker, (Princeton University Press, 1969).

Singh, H., *Village Leadership - A Case Study of a Village, Mohali in Punjab* (Jalandhar: Sterling Publishers, 1968).

--------"Basis of Village Leadership - A Case Study", *Khadigramodyog*, 14, No.8, (May - 1968).

--------"Community Leadership - An Analysis", *Adivasi*, No.2, (1966).

Singh, H., (1968) *Authority and Influence in Two Sikh Villages*, (New Delhi: Sterling Publishers, Pvt. Ltd., 1976).

Singh, Indra P., "Leadership in a Sikh Village". In *Leadership in India*, edited by Vidyarthi, L.P., (Bombay: Asia Publishing House, 1968).

Singh M.P. and Mishra R.P., "Characteristics of the Emerging Village Leaders", *Interdiscipline*, Vol.10, No.2, (Summer, 1973).

"Scaling the Determinants of the Emerging Leadership", *Interdiscipline*, Vol.10, No.3, (Autumn-1973).

Singh, S.N. and Arya H.P., (1966), "Value Orientations of Local Village Leaders". In *Studies in Rural Leadership*, edited by Udai Pareek, (Delhi: Behavioural Sciences Centre,).

Singh, S.N. *et al*, "Different Types of Local Leadership in Two North Indian Villages". In *Studies in Rural Leadership*, edited by Udai Pareek (Delhi: Behavioural Sciences Centre, 1966).

Singh, Vijaya Pratap, *The Evolution of Rural Stratification Systems in India, (1930-65)*, Ph.D. Thesis submitted to the University of Wisconsin, 1970 - *Ph.D. Dissertation Abstract*, p.5540. A.DAI 31 N.10.

Singh Y., "The changing power structure of Village Community - A case study of six villages in Eastern, U.P.". In *Rural Sociology in India*, edited by A.R. Desai, (Bombay: Popular Prakashan, 5th edition, 1978).

Sirsikar, "Leadership Pattern in Rural Maharashtra", *Asian Survey*, 4, (1964).

--------"Political Role of Panchayat Raj", *Economic and Political Weekly*, Vol.1, No.14, (1966).

-------- "*Sovereigns Without Crown*, (1973) (Bombay: Popular Prakashan,).

--------*The Rural Elite in A Developing Society*, (1970) (New Delhi: Orient Longman Ltd.,).

Solon T., Kimball and Marion Pearsall, "Event Analysis as an approach to Community study", *Social Forces*, Vol.34, (October - 1955).

Somjee A.H., (1971). *Democracy and Political Change in Village India*, Orient Longman.

Srinivas M.N., (1962) *Caste in Modern India*, (Bombay: Asia Publishing House).

--------"The Dominant Caste in Rampura", *American Anthropologist*, Vol.61(1) (February, 1969).

--------*India's Villages*. (Bombay, Asia Publishing House, 1966).

Srivastava S.K., "Directed Social Change and Rural Leadership in India". In *Emerging Pattern of Rural Leadership in Southern Asia*, edited by Dube, Leela, (Hyderabad: N.I.C.D. 1965).

Stogdill, R.M., "Personal Factors Associated with Leadership - A Survey of Literature", In The *Inter Study of Leadership* edited by Brown and Cohn, (The Inter State Printers and Publishers, Inc., 1959).

"Leadership, Membership, and Organization". In *The Study of Leadership* edited by Brown and Cohn, (The Inter State Printers and Publishers, Inc., 1959).

Tannenbaum, Robert, Irving R. Weschler, and Fred massarik, *Leadership and Organization - A Behavioural Science Approach*, (New York: McGraw Hill Book Company, Inc. 1961).

Theodore Peterson, "The Social Functions of the Press". In *Mass Media and Education - The Fifty Third Year Book of the National Society for the study of Education*, edited by Nelson B. Henry, (Illinois, NSSE, 1954).

Thirtha, N.V., *A Comparative study of Gandhiji's Educational Ideas and the Government of India's Basic Education Programme - A Study in Values*, (Unpublished Ph.D. Dissertation, Stanford University, 1959).

Varma, S.P., Narain Iqbal and Associates, (1973). *Voting Behaviour in a Changing Society*, (Delhi: National).

Verma, R.M., "Development of a Tool to appraise Socio-Economic Status," *Journal of Psychological Research*, 6.

Vidya Dhar Mahajan, (1975). *Leadership of the Nationalist Movement*, (New Sterling Publishers Pvt. Ltd.,).

Vidyarthi, L.P., (1967). *Leadership in India*, (Bombay: Asia Publishing House,).

Wolfinger, Raymond, "Reputation and Reality in the study of Community Power", *American Sociological Review*, Vol.XXV, (October, 1960).

Wood, Evelyn, "Patterns of Influence within Rural India". In *Leadership and Political Institutions in India*, edited by Park, R.L. and Tinker-I, (Princeton: New Jersey, Princeton University Press, 1959).

INDEX

O

P

R

S

T

U

V

W

Y

Z